IT / Non-IT Recruiter Training To Become A Recruiter (Junior)

SHAKRUDDIN KHAN

Published by SHAKRUDDIN KHAN, 2024.

Also by SHAKRUDDIN KHAN

The Smart Way To Personal Finance Success
Goal Setting 101 Achieve More Goals Than Ever! Faster!
Blockchain Masterclass for Businesses and Corporations
Master Your Mindset & Brain Framestorm Your Way To Success
Manipulation Techniques: How Can We Influence People's Thoughts And Behaviors
Leadership How To Influence, Inspire And Impact As A Leader
Learn How To Create A Safe Working Environment For Your Team
Productivity Hacks For Easily Distractible Entrepreneurs
IT / Non-IT Recruiter Training To Become A Recruiter (Junior)

Table of Contents

Copyright

Copyright © 2024 by **SHAKRUDDIN KHAN**. All rights reserved. No part of this book may be reproduced, scanned, or distributed in any printed or electronic form without permission. Please do not participate in or encourage piracy of copyrighted materials in violation of the author's rights. Purchase only authorized editions.

It / Non-It Recruiter Training To Become A Recruiter (Junior)

Book Design by **SHAKRUDDIN KHAN**

About

In this Book, I will share with you all of the knowledge and insight I have picked up as an IT Recruiter working within an international environment. As far as I know by myself that an official IT language is quite dry and yes, even, boring and sometimes hard to follow for a non-IT person, I have tried to make this Book as easy to understand (using a lot of practical examples) as it is practically possible.

Thus, in this Book you will find an introduction to information about:

1. IT Fundamentals (such as hardware & software, operating systems, and project life cycle), which are essential for further IT roles understanding;
2. IT roles itself (key responsibilities, functions, and skills related to it). Each recruiter has to stay in close contact with the hiring manager to be able to identify his needs and each recruiter has to understand the market to be able to find a perfect match;
3. IT Technologies (incl. programming languages, frameworks, databases, deployments, and communication tools)
4. Some tips for conducting the interviews.

I sincerely hope that you will enjoy this Book on an ongoing basis and that it helps you be at your job not only efficiently but successfully.

Are you ready to jump into an IT Recruitment world? See you soon! And no worries, if you can't swim there yet, I have a lifebuoy with me.

Who this Book is for:

1. Beginners in IT Recruitments
2. IT Recruiters who would like to deepen their knowledge or simply would like to learn something new
3. Those, for whom simple "keyword" search method is not enough
4. Those, who would like to understand and IT word better to be able to do their job great and to succeed

Introduction To Applicants Selection - A 36 Feet View Of The System

Hello, everyone, and welcome to this chapter two point one. Select the right person for all I am recruiting. So in this chapter, the objective is going to be around recruiting. We know the objective for that Book. The objective is to recruit. A great person. For eyeteeth. Roll. OK. That hasn't changed its celebrity. We are looking for a great person for 081. We've already seen that. You have two components. We have a great person. And we have the I.T. rule, OK? And they go together. OK. Always for the wall together in that recruiting. We want that great person to be very good at the role we are going to recruit for.

OK, a great person in isolation doesn't really mean anything for us. What we're looking for is to fill up a specific role, a technical role in I.T. role. And we want someone who's going to be very good at filling that role for us. OK, that's it. So from that. We are going to take a step back in the process and we're going to be looking at how it would work if we were looking for something completely different, but it's actually quite linked, which is gold. OK, so say we are looking for gold. Say we are looking for gold and provided we are. So this is us. This is a recruiter. OK. Not a very good looking regulator, but nevertheless a recruiter and provided that recruiter right here is walking around in an area where there is, you know, gold. It should be pretty easy to find that gold, provided we have a gold detector.

All right, so let's imagine for a second that our recruiter right here has that gold detector with him and is walking in an area where there is quite a lot of gold. So provided we have the detector right here, it should be quite easy because all we are waiting for is we're waiting for a beep. OK, we are waiting for that thing right here to do. Beep, beep, beep, beep, beep. And we know there's a beep. Then that means we found gold. That's as simple as this, OK? Now, with the detector, with the detectors, there is no risk provided that detector right here, provided the detector right here is set up properly.

There is no risk to get something else and gold provided the detector is set up for gold. And it's set up properly, we don't have any risk of finding something else and it's not going to beep for something different than gold, OK? Therefore, we are pretty much with a detector like this. We are pretty much solving the number one question, which is how do I select the right person and how to avoid the bad, the bad uptick in the back people, the people I don't want to hire. OK, so we have to remember two key questions, which is how do I select? The right person and how do I? Avoid that, the bad ones. OK. Well, you know, if that stuff beeps. For gold and only for gold.

Then as soon as we are walking around this, we know we have that for sure, would you? OK, so the question for us is, how can we build a detector? You know, basically and instead of detecting gold, how can we build a detector that's going to detect the right applicants, which is what we are looking for. You know, all gold, basically. OK, so let's take that detector right here. Let's take it, let's take it apart, OK? Let's put it apart and let's just see how it's working. OK, so we're going to go and grab our gold as well. Let's go and grab our gold as well. Up. There we go. All right, so we've got our gold. And so how does that stuff work? OK. Well, it's pretty simple. Right here.

We have some sensors. OK, we have some sensors. And as soon as the sensors come across gold. They are sending. A message to oops, no, that's for Carinae, sorry, Apu, or Detector's Gone now. Up. I'm not going to be able to erase all this doesn't matter. We're going to do it with another color as soon as the sensors are found. They're sending a message to this part here is going to go beep, beep, beep, OK. Now. The sensors, the sensors here. They're guided by that device right here and inside that device, that's like the brain or most of the detector. We have some properties.

OK, we have some property, so what does that mean, the property is that. And so here we have a flow of information. We said, OK, so. These properties are right here. It's a freeload off the detector. With what he has to find, AK. So these properties are preloaded in the machine right here. To tell the machine what you are looking for and in the census and continuous information of the stuff that he's encountering and as soon as. The census finds gold, the machine would beep because of the properties, because of decay. It's going to react with the information from the census. So that's how it works.

All right, so now we know now that we know how it works and we can try and build one. OK. And we can see that the starting points where everything happens is here with the properties. OK, this is the start of the whole thing, because if the properties are wrong, then the whole thing is going to be wrong as well. OK, so we need the right properties, then we need some sensors. Just sense reality to give us information that we need a link between the two, which is the information flow, which is actually pretty easy to build. But if I summarize it right here. Once I've got the properties loaded properly.

Once I've got it. The senses. And then the flow of information between the two. And it's that easy. OK. Then it is dead easy to find gold, provided I'm walking around gold again. The difficult part actually becomes finding. Knowing where I go, where I walk? OK. That part right here, we'll take care of making sure it's actually good they're going to grab. OK. Now, when it comes to this part right here, the properties, it is pretty critical because if it's not done right. For example, instead of loading, you know, the properties of gold so gold, we could have something like, I don't know, purity, gold, purity, level of purity, the size of the nugget. You know, maybe like a five centimeter minimum or something.

And then all the properties that make sure that it is actually gold. But if it is not rightly done and instead we are doing something like. You know. Precious. Metal, OK. Now, precious metal is interesting because we are actually looking for what we're looking for. Is this right? We are looking for this, we are looking for gold, but instead. We've loaded our machine or detector right here. We've loaded it with the information that we are looking for precious metal. Now, what do we think is going to happen? Well, what's going to happen is that our. Machinery here might not even might, but will beep for any precious metal. So you could start beeping for an emerald. It could start beeping for a diamond. Is it what we're looking for? No, we're not looking for a diamond.

We're not looking for an emerald. We are looking for these things. We are looking for gold. But because we have said precious metal, that even if we've been a little bit more accurate than this, you know, maybe we've even said, you know, above five centimeters and a few other things. But because it's all about precious metal and there's no actual segregation between the metals, we've not been selective enough. We've not been accurate enough in our selection in our properties. Then we're going to be we're going to be beeping on this and we're going to be beeping on this as well and any other precious metal. And so if we actually are looking for gold, then we're going to hire essentially we're going to grab, you know, Covid an itinerary.

We're going to hire the wrong stuff. Right. So this property is absolutely critical. All right. It is absolutely critical. So if we are getting to now or ELITE recruiting and leaving the goal for a second on the properties, okay, so we've got properties. And here we have gold. OK, we're looking for gold. When it comes to recruiting. We are looking for the perfect. Sorry. We are looking for success. Person. For what? For the job, for the rule. That's what we're looking for, isn't it? So we still have a role and we have a successful person. All right. And the two work together. All right. So from that. We're going to have to define this. Property. Before we can then define. The successful person properly. OK. It was a way we're going to build our properties. We're going to define the role.

And then from the road, we're going to deduct. The successful person and what we're going to call this in our recruitment process right here is the applicant, the successful. Applicants. The sun. Important right here is on a successful applicant persona, which is going to be deducted from. The job description. So that job description is right here. Is going to help us. Define the successful applicant persona. OK, that's going to be step number one. That's going to be number two. All right. So that's how it's going to work. Perfect. Now we've got this. We need some census. OK. Remember, we also need the census. So. In all.

You know, gold example. So that's number one here. That's number one here. OK, in our gold example, it's all about detecting what the properties are. What it's going to be is the same, you know, the senses. The sensors are going to detect what. The successful applicant persona, and so for that, we're going to have instead of like an actual census, we are going to do some tests. So anal anal detector, which is not going to be like a machine like we had. We can have some tests. We can have some tests that are going to enable us to. Confidently say whether or not we have a successful applicant persona in front of us or if we don't have someone successful. OK.

And we remember what the successful applicant's persona is, is someone who's going to be successful at the job. Right. This is all linked. So we are going to take a test. If a particular applicant is going to be successful. Well, not at the job, and for that, going to create some good tests that are going to enable us to make these decisions. It's very simple. OK. Very, very simple. And then from that. Well, we're going to do the same.

So what we need then from that is. Like hair. We have a flow of information. It's the same here. And we've already got it right here between our test and our applicants or properties or whatever. We're going to have a flow of information and that flow of information. From the test. He's going to be what we call a scoresheet.

OK, so we're going to school or applicants with an objective. And as much as possible, fast. Manners. In order to quickly. And reliably. Assess. The applicants. OK. And once we are able to do this, then everything starts to fall together and it becomes pretty easy to spot the right applicants and the wrong applicants, and it becomes pretty easy to select the right people for our job. OK. So if I summarize all of this for us. We're going to start here with a job description. That's what we're going to see in the next chapter. Then we're going to move on with the applicant persona. I mean, the successful applicant persona I should put. OK, so the job description is going to. He's going to help us to create a son of the sex for the successful applicant.

And number three, we're going to create some tests. And these tests are going to be created. From the successful applicant for Senate. And then number four, we're going to tie everything together. With this call sheet, which is going to be all sensors and automation. To make everything quick and reliable. OK. And that's. That's all. Gold detector. For. I see recruiting. And for each of these, we can have a dedicated chapter. OK. And that's simple . It is going to be for you to build your detector. That's going to help you to select exactly the right people for your next I.T. role. OK, so that's all. That's the introduction for this whole chapter. You would see I'm going to guide you step by step in this whole thing. And yeah, it can be fun and it's going to be very, very simple for you to build all of this. So I see you in the next chapter.

Define The Job Position (Results Based Method)

Hey, everyone, welcome back to this training and in this chapter define the job position, so we've just seen how all Jentleson on this on this whole chapter, how not to take bad applicants. How do you find great applicants? We've covered the basics. And now we need to delve into defining the job position, which is basically setting up all gold detectors. That's all that's what it is right now. We're trying to put together a gold detector for the perfect applicants. So what you're going to see is going to be pretty easy. It's going to be a very simple one. But there is a very, very key concept that we need to grasp. And that's the purpose of this chapter. Right. So we are where we were. OK, so the objective right now for us is to build all the sorry for that.

It's to build the gold detector, OK, to build a gold detector. OK, and what school golfers, what is gold? Well, gold is. Someone. Good. At. The role? Yeah. That's how we define someone, a person who's going to be good at the rules. OK, so we will have two key things right here. Remember, then we have some applicants. And then we have a role that we want to fill. OK. We were recruiting for. And the ideal scenario is someone who is going to be good at it, who's going to be good at this, so the gold detector is supposed to beep, beep, beep, beep, beep, beep, beep, beep, beep, beep, beep. Is it what you are supposed to do? Beep, beep. When it encounters people who are going to be good at the rules, it is very simple.

So for that, we need to load our gold detector, we need to load the high. How can you say the operation system? You know, the operating system of the gold detector? We need to load it with the right parameter. We need to build the right operating system. So that's all we're doing right now. We are building the operating system of a gold detector and we are going to load it. The Parramatta. Now, the key question is how do we come up with these Parmeter? How do we come up with the right parameter for the gold detector? Oh, right. So there's two ways to look at this one. There's two ways to look at this one. The traditional way, which is fine, but it has its limitations and is a more modern way, which I'm going to show you.

OK, so traditionally, how do people load that gold attack? That was very simple. They list all the tasks that. They want the person to do it. And then try roughly to think all we need, someone like that. OK. And usually what they do is that they refer. And that's really key. They are going to refer to standards. Position. So what people do is that they list a bunch of tasks, so, for example, they're going to say maintain. Shopify. Sites. Build Shopify. Pages. Maybe they're going to put something like a train. New Dave. I don't know if a whole bunch of other stuff doesn't really matter at this stage. You've got the point, OK. The foam that they're going to say, all right. Perfect.

We need a Shopify developer. Because by analogy, that is the closest job that we have in terms of standard job position. OK, so in other companies or in other businesses or what's not? People refer to that kind of task. I usually don't buy a Shopify developer. Therefore, we are going to use that reference, which we're using by analogy, you know, analogy, analogy to others,

Of the business. Analogy to our previous company. Analogy to maybe another road we have in the company, which is going to be similar. OK, and what are we looking for? But the traditional approach he's looking for is, is that standard. You know, they're looking for that standard job position that's standard that we're going to apply.

And once we are, we grab that standard, then we recruit. For the standards. And you can easily see where things can go wrong with that. That there is no such thing. There's no. Chub. As standard. Or there is, there is, but not for us. OK, which job Commerson did. Ask yourself what kind of job? What jobs are standard? And you're going to see exactly where the tradition is. The traditional way of recruiting comes from. Factory. Yeah. Industry. We need a paper machine. Operator. We need a car assembly line. Operator. And it's easy to see why factories and industry in general developed standards. Standardized job position. It's because we have Henry Ford. We also have before that joined Taylor. We also have Toyota.

I'm not going to go into the history of, you know, the industrial revolution and all that, but basically, you know, the movement has always been to standardize as much as possible. You know, the production so that we reach a level of a level of production that has the same quality no matter what. And to achieve that, you need a standard in standard practices. In a standard job, you need standard operating procedure. All of that stuff. We're not doing that. We are recruiting. We're not doing any of that stuff. We are recruiting. We are recruiting people to complete a difference. OK, Bob, sorry, pop, pop. Completely different. What we're doing is we're doing I.T.. Recruiting.

We are looking for high technical skills. Changing environment. That's what characterizes what we do. Usually, if you're looking for that kind of job, you are in a changing environment. It changes all the time. The market changes, the technology changes, disruption all the time. So the jobs are never standard. There is no such thing as a standard. There is no such thing as a standard. What did we have, a Shopify developer? It doesn't, it doesn't work. It doesn't happen. There is not a single company. Not a single company. That has the same need. When it comes to your Shopify developer, you know, some companies are going to be focused on, you know. UI, UX. That's going to be your ecommerce store.

Some companies are going to be focused on features. And back in. Some of the companies are going to be focused on. Developments. And server speed. What's not, you know, what's not, although you can find these things, you know, pretty much all the time. In any Shopify developer, the job is always going to be different. Plus also some companies, you know, they might have, I don't know, Magento. On top of Shopify, WordPress. So the need is always different. The need is always, always, always different, which is why trying to clean Shonn and refer to these standard job positions is completely irrelevant.

It's never going to work and you're always going to miss some crucial part of your recruitment needs and therefore wrongly input the setting in your gold detector if you try to. So we think about things like this. So this this idea that you can list some task and you can refer to standard job, that some people when they do this training day, they will list, you know, every single technical job position, you know, Shopify developer, Magento developer, data analyst, the data manager operation, these thorough. It doesn't work. It doesn't work. So although it's great to use these terminology so that people sort of know what you're looking for. You know, when they're looking at job opportunities and everything.

Thinking about things like this is doomed, absolutely doomed. And now we're going to see why and specifically how. We can create the job position and we can create and describe what we are looking for in a completely different way, that's going to make sure we are going to recruit the perfect person for us, and we're going to specifically set our goal to take that with the right privato. So instead of you going to remember that here, we started right here with the task. That was our starting point, OK? Well, we're not going to start this task. Instead, we're going to think about it. . Results. And KP. Ippei stands for Key Performance Indicators. I'm going to write it right here. That's his key performance.

Indicator. Basically, the question you ask yourself is. What results? Does that person. Need to achieve. OK, so your recruitment always starts. Somewhere, somehow right here with some kind of need, OK? And so the need can be anything. It can be your CTO moaning at you constantly saying, oh, we need more resources, we need more resources, we need more. We really need more resources. I need more resources. We're not going to be able to hit the deadline if we don't have more resources. That could be your CTO. It could also be simply your plan, you know, your plan to develop some features. And in order to develop these features, you need someone to do it. It could also be yourself. You know, you're drowning at work.

You are a dev by training as a developer, but you have too much to do. There's just too much to do. OK. It can be anything. You know, I could start going on and on and on and on and listing all possible situations and ways and this and that, that businesses end up needing to hire an I.T. technical role. But at the end of the day, there is a need somewhere. And that need is something very specific about it. It is vague. At that stage, it is vague, OK? It's vague. There's a vague need, and we're going to try to use a certain need, OK? And what people do try to ascertain the need is they're going to say, oh, for example, the seats come, come then and you need some money, someone. So are we going to say make me. The list of all the tasks.

That you might need. OK. And you can see how we quickly end up with a task that has a focus. And by the way, I did tell you about your city. Oh, yeah. Make a list of all the tasks and how much time you put on me. Nothing wrong with it. Nothing wrong with it. You can definitely start doing this. It's a really good idea to make that list. It's a good idea we're going to make here. It is a good idea. It's a really good idea, actually, to make a list of all the tasks and how much time it takes, roughly. And now we don't just leave it at that and look for someone based on this task. So although we can use that to ascertain the need, you know, ascertain the need right here. OK, so that step I will take step zero right here. OK. There is a need and someone manifest that need step number one.

We're going to try and ascertain the need internally. Maybe we're using it. The task list, you know. But then after that, we need to ask ourselves what are the results? What results are we going to want once we say, OK, right, okay, OK, we might need someone, OK, let's stick it here. There is enough to offer. Yes, it's true. We need someone to. Now it's. What about results? Result is what's going to be key. Okay, what results are you going to want that person to achieve? And there's only two different results. There are two different results. OK. There are two different results that we can achieve. Results No. One. Is oops. Is stuff that we achieve. So that's going to be, for example, profits. Of X sales of Y cost of that, OK, so we're looking for numbers. Plus, time.

So let's get all that in six months. OK, if we don't achieve something, we want to reach a certain number, whatever it is, for certain stuff in a certain amount of time. That's number one. Achievement results. These are achieving the stuff we want to achieve. And the second result, which is quite often the typical result we are looking for when we are looking for item equipment, is build. Stuff that we want to build. All right. OK, so that could be infrastructure. That could be websites. That could be some page. Doesn't matter what it is. OK. In. Time. So that could be six months, that could be one year, blah, blah, blah, blah, blah. OK, so we want to build a new website in three months. We want to build a new this inex. We want to blah, blah, blah, blah, blah.

OK. So that's always. Bill, OK. And we can have, we can have defined Bill, you know, we can have, for example, you could divide your year in a 90 day cycle and for each cycle. You will have your stuff to build and your timing. OK. For that new position doesn't matter. The point is we are either going to achieve some stuff or we are going to build some stuff. And that's what that person is going to do. All right. So these are the results. OK, so once we have defined the results. So what we want to do at that stage is have to choose three sentences. They're going to be results oriented, so either achieve. X by time.

We'll build. X by time and the difference here is that X, Y, here it has a number. It's a number of stuff, OK, it's X percent of profits, you know, it's one million sales. It has got a number on it, whereas build doesn't really have a number, but it has a defined stuff that we're building. OK. So that's what it is. And once we've done that, we have two to three sentences, as I said, that are two to three. I should have said the results. Sentences, I can also say KPI sentences, because once you've recruited that person, OK, these sentences right here. That's it. You don't need to create KPI for that person because you've got them. They're right here. OK, so you've already got pretty much your

performance review organized. You've pretty much got, you know, any bonus scheme that you want for job performance. If you do one, that's all so organized because you've got, you know, straightaway what you're looking for. All right. And that is our results. Now, from that result, what we're going to do, Willy, is that we are going to deduct. The tasks. Here are the two tasks. Okay. So. In order. Two, and you insert your. Without. Sentence one. We need it. Shoot. And then you will have. Your list of tasks right here. Both. In order to build a new website by 90 days, in 90 days, we will need to create new pages installed, a new X and Y chapter, blah, blah, blah, blah, blah, blah, blah. OK. That's during that exercise.

So for each. Results sentence. You want to do three tasks. And you might have some task that others say, you know, maybe some tasks are going to come up two or three times or whatever, it doesn't matter. But the point is, for each of the result sentences, OK, for each of your result sentences, they're here. Your result sentence you want. You want to read three of these tasks. OK. You want to hear three of them. So at the end you will have something like this. Just to make it clear. You will have. Results. Results No. One, and then you will have. Tasks. One, one, one, two, one, three. But in carrying on with the Matute task. She won choo choo choo three and so on and so forth. I kept. And that's how you get it done. OK, so that will help you.

This exercise will help you tremendously in number one, her focus. On the key tasks. The key task of the one that tied. Two results. No, to really understand. Who? Sorry. Not at the stage. Pop. What needs? Suing for results. Especially, as we said, the environment changes all the time. New technology comes and disrupts market changes as well. And everything we might you might be one of these companies especially that operates on this sort of 90 days window. Now that. One key, if you want them, you know, one key thing for you is going to be. Adaptability. If you really make the effort to map out. What are going to be the results? So if you're one of these companies that build through a 90 days plan and you already have some ideas of what you're going to build through the year.

You're going to be stuff that is different through the years, therefore you're going to need someone with different sets of skills and you're going to be adaptable. Who's going to need to learn new things when he's with you? He's going to get the idea. So it's very, very key in an environment that you make that effort. And you really defined these results right here. And you use his results to define exactly what's going to be what's going on in doing, because a third thing is that you're going to be able to cross off. All the tasks. If they're not needed, and that is really what separates great recruiting from average recruiting is that average recruiting they recruit for, as we said before, a standard job.

That has a lot of these. And some of these are what we are doing. We are doing a custom job, you pretty much create your own job based on the result that you want to achieve. So you're going to have a lot of them. And none of that so all your recruitments are going to be around the tasks that are essential to do to achieve the results. So you're going to be looking for someone who's going to really be good at these tasks specifically. Not all of these. All right. And you can see now how things are going to pan up. The next step is that we are going to start. And that's going to be the next chapter looking at what. Kind of person. Will. Achieve. These results.

And the kind of person who's going to be able to do it's going to be the best at achieving these results. Right here, whoops. It's the kind of person who's going to be very good. Are taking these tasks. Is it that these tasks are well defined and we get someone good at these tasks? The results are going to follow naturally. OK. So. Right now for you to do, you will see in the

Book just after that chapter's, there is a link to a file, an Excel file. You're going to open the file. I would also record a video for you to show you exactly how we fill up that file, but do now. One, get the file, get the Excel file.

Below the chapter. Number two, open Internet. And fit it. With your. Here's your results. And then your tasks. And only once you've done that, you move to the next chapter. Which is. Applicant persona. OK. Which is the final stage in building the gold detector. OK. We still know that gold detector and applicant persona is basically going to translate. So that's a gold detector. An applicant persona right here is basically going to be around translating these into a human being. I'm going to see how we do that. OK, so do that now. Do the do now. Right now. And I will see you in the next chapter.

Define the Applicant Persona

All right, everyone, welcome back to this training. We are now progressing on to loading up all the good detectors. We're looking to visit and build our Google detector. I'm going to write about it here. A gold detector. We are building that cool detector and we're looking for someone. Who's going to be good? That's a job for plain and simple, someone good at the job. OK. And these two really work together and that goal detector is going to go beep, beep, beep, beep, beep, beep, beep, beep, beep, beep, beep, beep, beep, beep, beep, beep. When we come across someone who has reasonable chances to be very good at the job we are recruiting for. OK, so we are building the gold detector, so we are looking at the building. We're building the operating system, we're building the intelligence of that gold detector.

The operating system, the brain, whatever you call it. We are building that. And we've already done quite a few things we've already done. And you should have it done right now in your access factsheet that I've given you. You should have already got the results. You're going to be looking for because you've done the chapter just before, which was around, you know, how are we going to define the job? And we've seen we moved from just a list of tasks and the sort of typical standard job position, which we saw was coming from the industrial era where people were running factories and therefore was the same job. And it's not.

So we've got all this and we've moved to a results based approach, OK. So you should have two to three KPI or result sentences. OK. So you should have them right here. You should have number one. You should have a . And you should also have number three. If you have more than you know, all the Marea, you can have more. It doesn't really matter of Ju-Ju three, because, you know, Liddie, people should have two to three KPI. But if you have four or five, it's OK as well. All right. So with that, I have also asked you to start putting the tasks, OK? And you should have three tasks for each KPI. So we should have task number one. One, number one, two, number one, three.

She won choo choo choo, sorry, three, and then we won. Three, two. Oops, three, three. So we should have all of this, OK? Oh, writes. So you should have all these done now. Define the persona. It is all about. A very special Hoopes, very special person right here, someone, OK? And so what we are going to be doing is very simple. Are we going to look at all these tasks? Remember the results at the back in and think what? Coins. Of person. Will. Number one, be good. And number two, enjoy. These tasks. So that's simple. So we're looking for someone who's going to be good and we're also going to enjoy these fabulous things. We usually go hand in hand with someone who's good at some task, someone who's taking certain actions, usually because they enjoy doing them. I suppose so.

What do we need to do? So what do we need when we're taking actions? So the task we're going to say. Taking actions. In order to take action, what do humans need? OK, so if I want to throw a ball, then I need certain things or ethnologists probably say I'm a basketball player and take a shot and I want to score some points. I'm going to need to take some actions in order to, you know, take the shots and make it. Now, I'm going to need to move around the court. I'm going to cover the ball. And then HBO Pernor is going to take the shot. And after a year of training in order to make a shot. So there's a range of actions that I'm going to need to take or be able to take.

These horrendous kids are going to need it. And we can usually break these things down into three categories, OK? We're Sullivan usually, so we can break these down and use three categories, number one of attitudes. OK. So if I want to make shots at basketball, I'm going to have to be cold blooded. I'm going to have to be calm. I'm going to have to be the kind of person who enjoys scoring lots of points, you know. I'm going to have to have that sort of attitude, OK? The number two thing we need is some skills.

You know, at the end of the day, I need to have had the right training in order to perform the move of taking a shot at basketball, receiving the ball, having the right skills to be able to move around the court fast and in a quick way that loses as my defender being able to navigate through screens, all that sort of like technical stuff, OK? So we need some skills. But I also need one last element, and that is knowledge. I need to be able to understand when they call a coach, so he calls some particular set. I need to know these sets. You know, when my captain or my teammates are telling me to do something specific, like set a screen or what I need, you know, what these things are.

If I don't know, I'm going to be lost on the court and I won't be able to score points. So these are the things. So just give it away. You know, if I am to say, we were talking about Shopify developers just before I let you know, Shopify, you know, knowledge and each has some knowledge of Shopify. I need to have some knowledge of the code of Shopify, which is liquid. I also need, you know, some other codes, potentially, maybe a bit of Magento, maybe a bit of steam in the middle of Java, maybe whatever. I need to have some skills which I need to be able to code. I need to have the knowledge of the code, but also be able to apply it to certain situations. So I need to have some skills in a coda. OK.

And attitude. I need to be someone who's patient. Maybe, maybe I need someone analytical. Maybe in that particular business. I need to really work as a team. You know, there's some businesses where developers work in silos and work together. They work by themselves in their GitHub repository and they put the folks in the CTO checks. And it's all very well. Well, in that particular business, that's going to be two or three people because it's a very complex project. So I need to be able to code with other people looking at my code and interacting with my code and whatever on each kind of attitude, team play or whatever. OK, so attitude, skills and knowledge, OK. And so we do have all. We have elections.

OK, they have an orange. And we also have our results right here in black. So if it is simple news. For each action, I need some attitude and some skills. A simple truth three. Two to three. Full. Each chapter. So I've got to act one on one, and I'm going to have a particular attitude. One point, one point, one all that, I also need a particular skill for that action. One point, one point of view. And that's it. I don't need anything else that is actionable on Bachu. I'm also going to need that attitude. But also one on one site. Bloops. Point to. And the same skills. And that's it. And then the last attitude, the last action, all the attitudes are here. But I just need one additional knowledge. All right. Carry on.

Two point one. Point one. She, for example, on one point two and so on and so forth, and then at the end I should have a list of probably you're going to have to choose three attitudes. And maybe choose kills. Three pieces of knowledge. Something like this, you will see at the end what you get. OK, lots of stuff is going to repeat itself. OK. You don't need to worry about this or you need to put a plus here. I forgot to put it so I agree with you. One plus one. Plus, I had another one. This one had one. So every time you repeat that, teachers, kids just put a plus. OK, so you know, OK. And so. Once you do this. Oops, sorry, once you do this, you're going to have a list. From top.

Truly, most important, to least important. And obviously, the one with the most plus are the ones that are the more important. So right now, at one point, one, one, two, one, one, one, one. One. And so on and so forth. OK, now this is very simple to understand, how are we going to do this? You know, are we going to take each of the actions, assign some messages for each of these actions? And after that, we can't point to everything. And it's all very simple, difficult because this is to understand what each of these things are. OK, so for that, I have listed you will see there is a list as a bonus. I think it's in the bonus if it's not the bonuses just under this chapter. There is a list. There's already a list that's already there. Off of attitudes. Scales. And knowledge.

OK. The thing that people struggle the most and it's the hardest to comprehend is the attitude, OK, so the attitude, I will say, if you don't know what you're doing and if you struggle, just usually use my privilege list, OK? Now, I am a bit tempted. I agree. But for you to start getting a grip, if you're new to recruitment, just use Prebble, it's going to. Is going to enable you to make fewer mistakes, OK? The skills and the knowledge, however it's oratory skills, is what people know. How did you do it? So she's action based. And knowledge is just knowledge. You just know stuff that you know, OK, so you might know about liquid coding.

But you might not know how to code. Probably a bad example, but you get the idea, OK. If I was to take, let's just take a non-technical so here would be a football fan who knows tons about football. They can't play where he is. Your football player. For that distinction. OK. It's not the same. All right, so have a bash at it. Use. Use that attitude sheet for the attitude, the skills and knowledge. You should know what you're doing. And once you've done that, you'll start to see that. You're traditional. And this is where, you know, it's really key that training is that your traditional I'm going to be sorry because I'm going to be a little bit rude. Your traditional recruitment.—. Which is a team player. Proactive. Initiative. Smile.

Energetic. You know, who wouldn't want that in their company? Of course, they want more than that company. That's just a lot of tussle, isn't it? No. Instead, we're going to be a lot more specific with our attitudes. You know, these are all if you think about it, these are all attitudes. That's why I always say attitude is a bit difficult, because there's so much—around the attitude, you know, team players on this, a lot of energy is going to really bend with the team if you have the right culture and attitude. Yeah. OK, great. That's called a great employee. OK.

Now, what is the actual attitude that you really need to deliver results? Because to be honest, without being lazy and not not judgmental, but the caricature is your your typical developer who, you know, sometimes people think of, you know, like the Big Bang Theory kind of developer, you know, like with glasses and introverts and in his cave plays too much video game and whatever, that kind of developer, maybe that's what you need. You know, he doesn't really like to talk to people or he doesn't have much energy. He is more than he thinks. Everything is so difficult to build and he shows so much. Well, actually, that's maybe that developer you need, because maybe you're building an app or something very complex that has a lot of risks.

And you need someone who's going to say, hey, guys, we're building something that doesn't make sense. We are building something that doesn't have the right code. You need someone who's absolutely Alsea about details and communicates it maybe in a very awkward way to the team. But actually, we don't really care if he's awkward as long as he communicates these things properly. OK, so we can leave all that H.R. recruitment to whatever—. And you're going to use a list of buildings for you and you get a focus on the actual attitude that you actually need in order to be successful. And if you do that and you do it properly, like I'm going to show you in the access in the Excel sheet, I've also added job training. You're really going to make a job description that is going to make a lot of sense, OK? So do that. Do it right now.

Now is the time to do it. Oops. Let's take the black black ink. All right. So you've got what you do now. Which is incredibly simple, is number one, you want to choose three. Attitude, skills. Knowledge. Fraction. OK. And three. So the three shoes. Here is the attitude list. And then three, join me in the next chapter, which is about putting together the job, the job ad, and also it's a test. The test. Housing is just one step to proceed. We've got to create some tests. And that's going to be our census, because now you have actually built that congratulation. You have built your gold detector. So that coal detector now. He's built. The operating system, sorry, the operating system. His belt and now we are going to create a test, so we're going to create now. The census, so once you've done all this, the operating system is done. We just need to create a census, and that's in the next chapter.

Creating Questions and Tests

And welcome back. This is it. We have actually built our gold detector, the gold detector is built. We are right here looking to recruit. So we have our gold detector, which is our main tool to recruit someone. Good for our job. Very simple. All right, someone who is good at the job. All right. And so for that, we have a gold detector and we have just seen the previous model finish the Soviet light blue. The operating system. ACase operating system. We now know exactly what we are looking for. OK, so that is done, that is built. And now, if you remember, we need to build the fences. The census so that all the Tector can go beep. Beep, beep, beep. When we have someone who does a job, that's it, that's very simple.

So we have the operating system now. We have the intelligence, we have the brain. So our goal detector knows what he's looking for, but he doesn't know how to look because he doesn't have sensors. OK, so we need the sensors. So right now, as it stands, we could be walking on the beach or walking on a goldmine and pointing to a detector or detector would know what to look for, but he wouldn't know how to look OK. He wouldn't it wouldn't be able to sense its environment in order to detect what he's actually looking for. So we need to help our detector to do that. And that is precisely the reason why we're going to be building questions and tests. All right.

So what are we looking for? So you remember that let's call black ink. OK, so you remember that ultimately we're looking for results. Okay. We're looking for someone who's going to be good at the job. That is someone who's going to be able to. Deliver. Deliver the results, OK, and these results. We've used them in order to build in order to deduct a link with some actions. OK, pop, pop, pop, pop, pop. The results have enabled us to say, hey, they're actually a list of actions, that if we take these actions well, we're going to create the results. OK. And that's someone. He's going to be good at taking them. He's going to be good and he's going to enjoy it. The actions.

Yeah, that's what we did last, just a model just before, you know, someone is going to be good and enjoy this action. So he's going to deliver as a result because he's going to be good and enjoy these actions. And the last thing we had. Where we're going to do that like this. Loops. So wrong color to start. There are red attitudes. Attitudes. We have some skills. Yepes. And some knowledge. All right, and so we. Yeah, or someone right here is still looking for that, someone right here. What's going on with my board is doing something I don't like, something a bit crazy. We are back. Excellent. So that's that someone right here. He's going to possess. These things. Right here.

Possess. He possesses things like attitude, skills and knowledge that we have defined the case so we can have probably two to three. Is three to three, maybe more doesn't really matter. Here we have. G3 three. And then Chukchi Sea, poor results. OK. And opportunities for here to just be here, which is hard to see here because we have Chuji, three of them factions, technically speaking, do you remember that? OK, so that's how it works. OK, that's how well, that's basically the operating system of our detector. So what we are now ultimately looking for is this. So that's what this is, what that's action and results. In a person. In a person. OK.

And so if we could find the person who's going to say to us, yes, I do have these attitudes, yes, I do have these kids, and yes, I do have this knowledge, and that would be 100 percent true. Well, we wouldn't need sensors because that is essentially what we need. OK, so if we if we could have a person telling us that we have these attitudes, skills and knowledge and that this and we never know where that person would never make a mistake in assessing their own attitudes, skills and knowledge, then we wouldn't need the sensors because we would just go around and ask who has these attitude, skills and knowledge? And these people, we raise their hand and we wouldn't need a sensor because they would be right.

They wouldn't lie and they wouldn't be mistaking their own abilities. But the problem is that people sometimes lie and do it very often. I would say they misjudged their own ability. OK. And also, quite a lot of the time, people think that we are wrong as recruiters and maybe they can learn on the job when they really colts' and this and that. So for that reason, we need to question and test. So we need our senses. OK, so. What are we going to question in THETH where these very things are? OK, we're going to test and question the attitude, skills and knowledge. So I always try to make a distinction between questions and tests, and you should do the same, OK? And in fact, we are going to talk about tests and questions. OK, so what's the difference between test and question? What tests are things that we do mostly? In the questionnaire.

OK, so we're going to have a question and people are going to reply to a questionnaire. And so in that phase, people can use it. I'm going to be broad here, but let's say that they can use Google. They can Google the answer. There's no way when we create a questionnaire and people take the questionnaire unless we create an assessment center, which we can do. But let's just say let's just keep our feet on the ground and say we're going to have an online questionnaire and people are going to fill the questionnaire so that we can see whether or not they are that good. They're going to be able to use Google. OK. So for that reason, anything that could have a skewed answer because people can use Google and therefore they can find the answer.

If we don't want them to do that and it is only from some specific stuff that we don't want them to do, then we cannot use the test. OK. So if we can use Google, if use of Google is OK, it's OK. We can use Google, then the test, the test is the greatest perfect. And there's even some tests where you want them to use Google. You want them to show that they can go and look for the answer if they don't have it. OK. So that's all good. However, if Google. It's a big no no, we don't want them to use Google. OK. Therefore, we're going to have to ask some questions during the interview. Because during the interview you will be able to see whether they are thinking on their feet or whether they know the answer already or whether they are trying to be sneaky.

I have a sneaky look at Google. OK. And anyway, if you're face to face on zoom, you can't just have the sneaky Google. It's just looking up. You're going to see whether they know or not. OK, so. Technically speaking, you will want to test. Knowledge. At the end with some questions. OK, if you ask questions in the test, then they can use Google and you won't be able to test whether or not they've been able to find the answer. And if you want people to find the answer, then that's great. But if you really want to look at knowledge, let's say, for example, I'm just going to take a really broad example here. But you want to recruit a nuclear physicist.

Well, if you ask some questions about physics and nuclear physics, whatever, in the tests, someone could look at you. Now, granted, the question is very, very complex. And you will see straight away. Usually someone who really doesn't know it just copied an article. OK, but if you have some broad question about the topic, someone very clever can effectively go on Google and provide you with an answer that you think actually that could be the guy who could have the knowledge. But it doesn't have an MBA in nuclear physics, but it wouldn't be an MBA. It would be a master in science, whatever. It doesn't matter. You get the point. But that's the way he's delivered.

Interesting. Well, actually, he's just using Google. But if you have a question, then it's a discussion. It's a two way process. They can hide a case. So knowledge is right here. However, our friends' skills, the skills. Perfect for the test. Why? Because skills, it's about doing OK and reasonably speaking, if someone can code in liquid. We were talking before FPU, whatever it is, or Python, they're not going to learn to code in the 48 hours or mass, you know, as much. One week that they are allowed to fill up the test, OK. So even if they use Google to try and find some of how they can code in Python, reasonably speaking, it's not going to happen, it's just going to be too much for them to learn in order to be able to use it properly.

So you can reasonably test and let them use Google and all the resources in the world. The only thing that you need to account for is a sneaky, sneaky friend. OK. That's the only problem with skills, is sometimes people would actually use a sneaky friend, a sneaky friend. But, you know, if people do that, you're going to see straightaway in the first week. And it's not going to take very long. And, you know, he's one of those situations. It has happened to me once, but I was able to find out about this because I read some referencing, which is something we will do as well. You know, if you do some referencing and you contact previous employers and Avvo, everybody has experience in coding.

What you can see straight away, you know, as you work with this person is coding. No, I didn't. All right. Interesting. So and then what happened in that specific case is that I mentioned Rudell, the fact that they've actually used a friend, a sneaky friend, Mike, here to use a tacit that they asked and that they did very, very well. So anyway, long story short, if you're referencing. Yeah. You can cut on this, the sneaky friend right here, but a test online test for skill is perfect. And then the last thing we have is attitude. Now, attitudes are very tricky to test. They're very tricky , which Suketu questions. So we are going to have to put them in the middle. We are going to be able to test for some attitudes with some tests here.

Some of the hostages we're going to have to ask some questions for are going to have to have an interview. OK. But the other thing we can do with knowledge, which is right here, which we've put around a question, because if you want to ask question of our knowledge, you're going to have to ask and doing the interview what we can you what you can also do at that stage right here and test is, is is is knowledge right here. You can test it with. Qualification. Certification. OK, so I will give you an example. Let's just say, for example, that we want new recruits. I did that, actually.

Recently, I'm going to use that example, because quite a simple one in an accountant's, okay, I was looking for an accountant and I wanted him to have knowledge of a specific software, which equals zero. You might know about it. It's specific accountancy software. Only then to have a good knowledge of Xero and be able to do some light programming on it. OK, like programming on the way. You can do some live programming on Xero, OK? So it was sort of I on plus plus with life. So I like programming skills. OK, so very simple. Zero. They have certification. OK. So instead of going through and creating some test about zero or whatever I just said, you need to be certified. OK. Has some certification.

I want you to be accessible. Certified. Same thing, for example, if you want. You might have, I don't know, a customer service team. OK. Customer service, technical, the technical, the very technical. And you're selling a fleet of all Microsoft products, OK? You sell Microsoft products like I don't know, like cloud cloud solutions for professionals, like for big, big enterprise enterprise, Microsoft products. So you're looking for some technical customer service people. They need to have some knowledge of Microsoft, where Microsoft, they do have their own certification. So it's very simple. You need to be Microsoft certified in cloud solutions. OK, and so on the CD, I want to see that certificate, if I don't see it, then you have the knowledge or I can't test that you have the knowledge properly, therefore, I'm sorry. But it sounds very simple.

OK, so knowledge can actually be tested by here. And skills, we can definitely test them right here and an attitude some can be tested here, some and knowledge right here, OK. So this is how it's going to pan out. Is that. Our recruitment process, and this is our senses. OK, so our sensors for the gold detector are our process for recruiting. And so what we are going to do is we are going to choose the people that are going to come. OK. People are going to come from all angles right here by five, OK, and they're going to get their CV. OK, we're going to get their CV path. OK. And in their CV, we're going to then send you a questionnaire. And in our questionnaire, we can have some, especially some tests. We can have some tests, OK? And these tests we're going to have.

And so these tests are going to enable us to obviously reveal the attitude. And then test the skills. And potentially, Of course, knowledge, which is going to be very simple, it's all going to be around, you know, certification and this and that, OK. So what we need to do right now is basically focus on this one. OK. Why? Because they're the most difficult skills, to be honest with you, the skills. You wouldn't know exactly what you need to test and how you need to test them. And you can be very, very creative for these, OK? So when it comes to the skills, what you want to do is create a real life situation, OK? So I'm just going to give you an example quickly.

Real life situation, OK, so for example, right now, just right now, and which is probably why also I've talked a lot about my Shopify of. I'm actually recruiting. I'm creating a Book. I'm recruiting with my own consulting for a Shopify developer. I'm looking for a Shopify developer. OK. So he needs to be able to both the front end. And the back end, so he needs to be able to code as well as have some UI, UX and do stuff that are not too ugly. OK, so what I'm doing for that, I've created a test and the test is very simple. I have a Sigma Alpha Sigma. Is this sort of. I don't know if it's a program, a soft touch, but I was at a meeting about this thing on the Internet, you can check Sigma where you can create page designs. OK.

So I've got to say, she's created a pastry's island sigma, and all I'm asking the developer to do is put it in code. It is created on Shopify. So we've got this design on Fima and created on Shopify and the whole thing, which Ivan told the developer, but I'm expecting I could develop the kind of people that I want to hire for the company to really pay attention to. You know, mobile friendly. So we need to have some sort of seamless transition between laptop and mobile. And the element, the way I've done them and everything they are, they're actually quite difficult to code properly.

OK, so I've actually asked a CTO of the company I work with for the recruitment to create me a test that's a bit difficult geocode really, you know, it's a little bit difficult to code. And so what we do as well is use a GitHub repo. So that Micheel right here, who's helped me to create a task, can just check, check the repo, download everything, install it and see how it's looking like and everything and. OK, so it's very simple, you know, on the face of it and tribalists. My guy right here is Klyn. I don't touch you. Me for good, for good developer. It should take, you know, 30 minutes, maximum one hour.

It's a one I would test, OK. Nothing else but 30 minutes to an hour, a maximum for someone who's good at what they do to be able to do it. So with that intelligence as well, I can ask, was it on the test? I can ask in my interview, how long did it take you to just test, you know, just for every interview question. How long did it take you? I don't want to take you to that test, OK? How long did it take you to do that test? Very simple. And I guess, you know, if I'm within that range and I'm happy, then I have to think about it. OK, so that's how it's going to work. Now, what we want to test as well are the attitudes, OK, so that cricket tests, let's not kid ourselves.

They are tricky to test, OK? So. I'm going to. I've made it very. I could go on and on and on about the logic and everything and this enough, but I'm going to have an interview chapter to really explain to you how you can do an interview and everything and do it properly. OK, so we're not going to worry about this. These things are tricky to test. That's why I've created a resource. You have a resource. And you have a sheet with all the attitudes, the examples and everything, and you have the test as well. OK. So in my sheet, you have the right to use and you have to test them or which questions to ask when you have to choose questions. OK. So for some attitudes, you can go with a test which is good because you want to test as much as you can.

At the test stage, chief people who are as qualified as possible in the interview. But if you can't, then we're going to have to use a test during the interview to have some questions. I'm explaining everything with enough resources. It's an Excel spreadsheet. We have the list of attitudes and the list of how you can test for the actual whether it's a test, testing the question or this question. OK. So the attitude is very, very difficult. OK. I could spend my time creating a whole training around how to, you know, look for the right attitude and not worry about it. Is a resource and the resource is fully comprehensive. You just have to follow the sheet. And it's that simple. OK. Because otherwise I'm just going to lose everyone.

The training is going to be very. Going way too complicated. So attitude, you just use a sheet. OK. So. Now we can see that things are very, very simple, OK, so we get to recreate the senses. OK. And we are at the do now already. Look at that and do now. So you need to create your test. And in that test, you're going to use your attitude. And you just follow the sheets. You test the skills. You're going to put together a real life test. Like I've explained with the stigma and the Shopify page and everything and knowledge. Well, knowledge is simple, it's a diploma. Certification.

Qualification and God knows. OK. Now, I know that in our industry, a lot of people think, oh, yeah, but you can learn you don't need a diploma or whatever, you can learn things if you really. Yes, but that's not going to help us. Testing. And we want to test things to get people who are qualified in the interview. So if. If the knowledge. Is actually a skin. Then be my guest and use a test, you know, you can use a test. If it's not actually a serious kid and it is just pure knowledge, you need to learn physics, you know, you need to learn computer physics or whatever, you need to have some good amount of knowledge of these things. Then you cannot be tested.

Therefore, you have to have the qualification. Qualification. Necessary. With the best will in the world, we are never going to be able to test properly if someone has a recollection that the students should have on physics or computer science or whatever. It's just not going to happen. So if your position is that technical and requires that level of knowledge, then the qualification is essentially, you know, that's all you can test. You know, you need to have a qualification that's that simple. Don't be afraid. Just standing your ground and asking for certification or qualification is perfectly fine. And yeah, some people are going to say, yeah, but you can look at identity, which is clear. Yeah, OK. You don't need to go to school. University. Up your points.

If it's a skill base and yes, you can learn the skills by yourself, doing some Books, whatever. And yes, I'm all for that. But at some point it stays in line. And that line is if the knowledge is such that you can't really apply the skills that you need to have that kind of general knowledge about stuff about a certain area like I don't know nuclear physics or computer science or data, for example, processing or whatever stuff like that. You're going to have to have some qualification at some points, and you need to draw that line and ask the qualification in that test, OK.

And once you've done that, basically it's the rest of the stuff you can't, you can't check at the test level, you're going to have just some questions. And I refer you to the interview chapter for this. We're going to see how we ask this question at the interview chapter. OK, that's the interview chapter. OK, so leave it for now. And you've created your test. You've done really well. Your test is ready by now. You can now jump into the next chapter. And as it stands, your gold detector has an operating system. INAH has some sensors. Well, we need to connect the two and we are going to go.

Create An Appealing Job Advert For Your IT Recruiting Process

Hello, everyone. Welcome back to this Book and we choose a final part of the very first final chapter, sort of as part of the Book, which is a job advert. So at this stage right now, you've got your gold detector. All right. You've got the gold detector. We're going to put it right here. Oops. Sorry, the gold. Detector the gold, then the detector is built, it says. It's got an operating system. We've done that. It's got sensors on it. It's got the sensors. All we need now is to connect both of them with some messaging, some kind of connection, whatever. OK, we just need to talk to each other. OK. And that is that he's missing, that we are going to see that in the next part of the Book.

Where we're going to see, you know, how we automate, how we automate everything, how we create our own system and everything. So we don't need to worry about it too much. Right now, we've got an operating system. We've got the sensors that go gold. They're ready to do beep, beep, beep, whatever he sees. He sees someone who is good at the role we are going to try to recruit for. Very simple. OK, so now we need to focus on the actual role. OK, because we are looking for someone. Good. At the roll. OK, so that we define starting with results. That's the starting results. And then we've done the persona. OK, we've done the persona of that person over here.

Now we are getting to writing our job adverts, and the job advert is really what I always call, you know, the bridge. It's a bridge between them and us. OK, so here we are. That's us. We don't lead to great pop. We some here and here are our targets, OK, up. And they really want to work for us. They look really competent like this. Uh, you know, make them blonde, actually. So this way we know, so this is the applicant and this is us. Well, you know, between the hair like this, how do we bridge this gap right here? That's what the job that's going to do is the job advert. He's going to see the job adverts and through the job advert, he's going to get in touch. OK, he's going to get in touch, so he's going to see it.

And he's going to get in touch, OK? And that's two very important steps right here in front of you. OK. Because what's going to happen is that that person right here, he's going to seize a job adverts. So that's step number one. Step number two is going to read it. The job adverts. And least at number three, he's going to get in touch. OK, so let me summarize this one for you one more time. Because that's pretty essential. OK, so there is us. These are our targets. Hoops with an arm. OK. Nevertheless, next year, our targets. OK. And in between. We have a job. Adverts. OK. And what's the target going to do? No one is going to see. The job adverts. Number two, he's going to read. The job adverts.

And I'm with three. He's going to get in touch. Slash applies. The interesting thing with this is that no one is seeing the job advert, OK, so that's what we're going to call the impression. So we're not going to call it an impression, I'm making a mistake here. Sorry for that. We're going to call it. These are the views. OK, because in order to have views right here, we actually need right here that zero impression. It's got nothing to do with him. That's got to do with us, like us. Our job is to go and impress our job adverts. OK, impression. So what I mean by that is that if our job advert stays, let's say. Here. Which is on a Google Drive or in our hard drive on a computer and doesn't go anywhere else. And right here, no one's going to see it. So we need to put our job advert out there in the public.

You know, we need to put the job adverts in places that are likely. To meet our target audience, the people want to recruit, OK, so they say, for example, I want to recruit a Shopify developer. I'm going to put my job advert in Shopify developer groups on Facebook, for example, not saying this is what I'm going to put it, but that's an example of a case for you so you can understand. So straight away, we're putting our job adverts in a Facebook group that's full of Shopify developers. That creates some impression. Of our job adverts and what's going to happen from these impressions is a number of people are going to see the job adverts. OK, so we're going to generate some views. We're going to generate some views right here. OK.

People are going to view our job advert. So that's number one. OK, so that's. Is right here. One key metric for us to track when we are recruiting, you know, is the number of U.S. The number of U.S. On job adverts getting now from these views. A number of people are actually going to read. But another one is going to actually drop. They're going to leave. They're going to land on a job advert. They're going to start doing as they are. This is a lot of—. I'm not lying to this. This is this. I'm not interested in this. Oh, this isn't just but it's not for me right now. I'm just going to leave. So I'm not going to read further. I'm just going to come in and as soon as I sit. Oh, yeah, no, that's not what I thought I was.

I'm off. I'm going, I'm gone. I'm off. So not everyone will read the judgment. Okay, now we don't have a metric right here, you know, unless you're running a very big website where you have some heatmap and a lot of technology to be able to know how many people have scrolled down and this and that and let us assume that you don't have that. And if you do, that's a bonus. You understand what I'm talking about. If you don't, that's OK. You don't need it. But what you need to understand is that a certain amount of people here are going to read it. That's going to be lower than the views. OK, and all a job in that step is to maximize. The views. Sorry, maximize. The number of red ratios. OK, so that's red.

Divided by views. As a percentage. We want to maximize that number as much as possible, so we need to make it. Well, that's one key thing, is that we need to make it appealing. OK, that's A14, right, because that's an election for us. It's got to be appealing. You know, we're going to have to show Oddjob adverts, but that's not enough. It's got to be appealing. It's got to be mouth-watering for people who are going to read it. It's got to be interesting. It's got to have a bang. It's got to be something that people want to read to learn more, because the more drop we're going to get right here, the fewer applicants we are going to get and the more they're going to cost us. All right.

And then after that, once people have read it, then some people, how are you going to get in touch? You know, they're going to get in touch, but Of course, lower than the people who have read it. So people are going to read the whole adverts and say anything, anything. It's really interesting, but that's not for me right now. So what I'm going to start reading, they're going to go halfway through the thing and it's going to have something else. Maybe save the baby starting screaming. And after 10, maybe their wife is asking them to go and buy some bread or some milk or I don't know what you know, lots of stuff can happen. So not everyone will apply.

OK, it's going to be lower than the reader and or key metrics right here are going to be application. Divided again by views. As a percentage, that's a pretty big one in this one, we want it as high as possible. This one is key. One is as high as possible. So in order to maximize these applications. OK. We want to be number one. Make it easy to apply. It's got to be easy to apply if it takes ages. Then people there in the moment, you know, you imagine a situation where someone is waiting for the child coming out of school. They are a park and maybe a place. They aren't really are not allowed to be tall, but they are just waiting for a kid. And they're hoping he's going to come out of the gate quicker than nobody he does because he's normally the last one.

But they're hoping that I've told him yesterday to get out of there quickly because I can't get to the park. So I'm hoping he's going to do that. And we're just waiting for the child. And why do we wait for the child, when we wait for the bell to ring, which is quickly going on the phone and we're looking at some job ads because, yeah, we fancy a promotion, we fancy different jobs. And who hey, there's this. I've just seen that ad right here as well. Interesting. I'm reading that ad right here. Oh, that's very interesting. And I'm clicking on apply and clicking on the opponent. But you know what? It's a complete page of. It's very, very difficult.

There's all these questions. I'm going to have to do it right now. You know, I'm hoping it's going to come out quickly because I told him yesterday to come out quickly. So I'm just going to drop by if it's difficult. If it's hard, if it's long. And cumbersome and we sort of question and they are Fifita, all these forms and everything, they're just going to drop. It's just going to drop, they're going to think, I'm going to do it later or I'm not going to bother with that, they want all this information, I don't want to do all this. You know, they're just going to drop. OK, so we want to make it easy to apply. Very, very simple to apply. Don't confuse people.

Confused quite often. I'm going to put it right here. OK, OK. I'm going to put it right here. Do not be confused. Do not ever confuse. Application. With. Selection. It's not the same thing as an application. It's pulling people, OK? It's getting people to apply, getting their email, getting their CV, that's what we want. A lot of application selection comes after one. They've been pulled in. Once we've got that email, then we can get them to fill out some form first and we can set up reminders and we can keep in touch with them and we can ask them again and again and again to debate and everything. We can set that up to have a lot of people filling up our phones.

But if we start selecting at that stage way here, when it should be simple and quick, and then are, you know, in that situation when they park where they shouldn't be, and the waiting with a kid coming out of a school and they've got these five or 10 minutes to kid and they're looking for a job, then whatever. If we select now, we're dead. We're not going to get anyone. It's going to be a disaster. OK, so we don't want to do that. The other thing that we don't do in the application. So we want to make it easy and we want to get, as I said, the e-mail. And the city, that's it. All we want is to send us an email with SCV and usually even on their phone, people are able to do that because they have saved their KBE on their message, on their Gmail of their own, on their drive or whatever.

So just sending us an email with a CV is very simple for them. So we can definitely ask for that. And that takes for people that take three seconds and in three seconds, they can they can they can apply and we can get that email. We can get the team in, and that team is absolutely critical. So if you're getting an application, don't just apply for the city, you've got to critique the event. So critical, because then with that, we can then send them with the information. We can then continue the dialogue with them. OK, so that's pretty that's how it works. And so the third thing is to get in touch, apply. We want to do it multiple times. OK. So throughout our multi, multiple, multiple time.

Throughout the job advert multiple times where people see this application, people have lots of lots, lots, you know, few times to the application whether they can have an opportunity to apply and apply simply. OK, that's freaky. All right, good. So from that. We understand the logic. OK, so no one is impressed. Number two, they're going to see it. They're going to read it. They're going to get in touch, OK? So we want something that's going to generate a lot of views. You know, that's going to be our job to put it out there to get lots of views. It's got to be appealing. It's got to be easy to apply. It's got to be with an email. We've got to make them apply multiple times and more than anything.

It's got to be, as I said, appealing, appealing, appealing. Appealing, simple. These are the things that are the case, so that's what we need to do. All right. So from that, we're going to get an actual thing because it's going to be a lot easier if we do that. OK, so. I'm going to take this color right here. So I was recruiting for a cause creator, to fill a position, but never mind. We're going to check it because it's always the same thing. So I always start my day. And these things convert very, very, very well. OK. The first thing you need to notice if I take a step back. Going to think about this is very long. You know, it's a very long copy. Well, it's not actually a long copy because you can see the width loops. Right here. In short.

And this here, right here is long. And you get to see what on earth are you doing this? Why would you have something very short with a whiff of this in a very long way here? Well, that, my friend, is because this is not right now. You know, it's not 2000 anymore, is it? You know, the 2000s are over. This is 20, 21. And as I said to you, we are parked in the wrong or in the wrong place where we shouldn't be waiting for the kid to come out of school, we got five minutes to kill on the phone. That's gotta be mobile first. It's absolutely critical that any of your job advertisements are absolutely mobile first. It's got to be mobile first. If you're not mobile first, if they have to scroll this way or this way and it's not clear and everything is, you know, in any place because it's mobile and you've designed it for a laptop or whatever, you're dead. You are dead. It is not appealing.

It's going to be ugly, is going to be awful, is going to be horrendous. It's got to be mobile first. You've got to design your stuff mobile first to Faraci. Either use, you know, a WordPress. You can use click funnels or you can use any stuff that you get that is easy if you don't have any of this technology, you can make calls so people can show you how to do it. But if you're recruiting, I'm assuming you have some basic knowledge of, you know, what Web recruiting, whatever, or Web design or whatever. If you don't find someone who does both, whatever you do, that job advert is gotta be mobile first. If it's not mobile first, you're not playing the game of 2021. You're you're you're you're with the dinosaurs in 2000 and you are dead.

All right. So mobile first, I cannot emphasize how important this is mobile. The second thing I said for five, ten minutes, killing some time, waiting for the bus, waiting for the kid from our school, waiting for the queue to clear at the post office, whatever. You know, it's got to load quickly. If you're using one of these things where, you know, it takes ages to load, it's not HTP as whatever, you're dead. You know, you're absolutely dead. This is a big no, no. It's got to be quick. It's got to be quick. It's got to load quickly. It's got to be steep, it's got to be, you know, two thousand and one ready. OK, so that stuff's got to load quick, don't put some big image that's going to take ages to load and everything, don't make something super complicated. It's got to load quickly.

It's got to be ica's and it's got to be mobile first. If it's not that you don't even write the sentence, you get that sorted first. OK, so that's a first. Second thing is. When they come in, they want to see exactly what you're talking about, so bam, you name the job. I know we don't like the standard. Job name, OK, when we define the job, when we define the job, we don't like that. That's OK. I've said it. We work, we work when results have things. But when we are talking to our agents, you know, they're not within our company. They don't know how we think and everything. And out there, everyone thinks around a standard job name. So when someone sees a job and they want to understand very quickly what it is about. So you've got to put a standard job name.

So if you're looking for, you know, a new developer and the main technology is going to be like Shopify, like it was sourcing before, or if it's going to be Magento or if it's going to be Java, then you put a Java developer, you make it simple, you put Java developer all you put Java, Magento 50/50. But you get the point you need to put something that people are going to understand very, very quickly. So for that, you use one of the standard domains. OK. Once you put that, I always put that chapter right here. It is a crucial chapter. OK, highlight. And we use emojis. Emojis are so important in recruiting emoji that enable you to create emotion. And a connection.

And also stand out. So straight away, someone who sees that S.Y. here, they're going to find it interesting and we can see what I'm putting here. I'm listing all the possible benefits, so benefits straight away. Benefits, benefits, benefits. So you answer the question straightaway, what's in it for me? That's the audience that's coming onto your job advertising, they want to know what's in it for me. The number one question that someone who's got five, ten minutes to kill and browsing some jobs is going to ask himself is it goes only to question the they're going to ask themselves, OK. So number one is how much is he paid? Number two is.

Is it right for me? Is it right for me? These are the two key questions. So if you can at least answer one of them in that chapter, why here in the first ten lines? That's a you can see written as a bullet point, super simple to read and everything with some good emoji to connect. Then straight away, that person is going to scroll down. I want to know more. OK, I want to learn more. So that chapter right here is absolutely creepy. We are going to grab their attention, and pull them down to look, you know, and read further. And also. You can see straight away we're not beating on the bush apply now being Bambu. OK, so straight away, we are aiming probably around five percent of people who read who are going to apply right here. They got five here to see that.

Wow. That's great. Tammam applying. Great. Excellent. Perfect. Maybe they're not going to be right. Doesn't matter. We're not, we're not selecting. We know we're not selecting anyone. We are getting a lot of applicants. What we're trying to do, we're getting a lot of applications. So then we are getting the traditional chapters around the job advertising case, so that's what I told you, these are the two questions that people want to know. How much does it pay? And is it right for me? And in that question right here, is it right for me? There are a number of questions they are asking themselves. The first question is, is it a job? Can I do it? We don't tell you. That's the kind of question, the essence of the job.

The second one is a company. Are they nice? Are they, you know, exciting? Lips. I was excited. Will I like them? And so on and so forth. OK, so people ask himself questions around the job, around the company and Of course, around career opportunities. So. We are going to answer all of these questions in our job, OK? And we progress chapter by chapter. So the first question is to introduce ourselves. It is literally like when we meet someone like. What gives a first impression is our look, this is what this is what we look like, this is our appearance, this is how smiley, well dressed and everything, we are OK. Now we are shaking hands. We're getting here. We've shaken hands right here. We shake hands and we introduce ourselves, so literally take it right here as we shake hands.

Hey, we are at the same conference. How are you today? OK, so we shake hands and we introduce ourselves. OK. So we want to create a short, snappy paragraph around, you know, who we are, the company I want to talk straight away about, you know. Omission. So what do we do? And of value. Which is who we are. Some people love that. People love a company with value, especially in 2021. You know, people want to want their work to be worth a bit more than just work. They want to be part of a project. They want to be part of something special. So your mission, your values, you put it out there and straightaway your earning points.

We want to keep an eye on the mission right here. It's always the same one to keep pulling down, keep putting down, keep the interest. So we want to build interest and build connections. There's only two things we want to do in this whole process. Always remember we want to build. The interest. Feel the connection. Connection is the emotion between us. Emotion between us. OK. That's why we have the emojis, that's why we have the emojis right here. That's why we have the values mission. So we build emotion, build emotion, build emotion. And we are also building interest. You know, we tell them about the money and tell them about the holidays.

We're telling them about the benefits, all the great stuff we're doing, blah. And we want to, you know, keep pulling them down, keep putting them down, keep putting them down and keep them to read, read, read. OK, that's what we are doing. Company hiring. So that's it. We've talked about the company. They know who we are. Great. Now, you know, we can put a little image here. It's always good. You know, put some images you don't need. You don't need you. Only a hundred of them. But just put an image right here. That's going to illustrate. Ideally, what they want. You know how they're going to picture themselves? I actually recruit for my own company, lots of digital nomads, simply because they work well for me, you know, for a lot of reasons, it's a good deal for me. I can access people who are very multicultural with that.

But you still share quite a lot of things from a culture standpoint. So lots of multicultural people who work since I'm potentially full time for me, who share similarities culturally, which means that they can be all around the world. I can have interviews running 24/7 by people who have lots of different cultural backgrounds. And for me, that works really well. So I always join in my advert, my own person. I guess I'm not saying you should do the same, but my own advert, I was put to death nomad, because that's the sort of lifestyle I try to sell them. I try to give to my employees. That's one of the benefits. And you can see if you read the stuff I offer right here. That goes with it. OK.

So a little picture is nice and easy, you don't need it if you don't want to put it, but it's always nice for a little picture to break things down. And then after that, we answer that question. We are still answering the question with or without that question. They want to know about the job. They want to know about the company and they want to know about a career opportunity. So here we go. We carry on. You see the jobs and responsibilities. We just highlight the job in a very simple way. You don't choose to do tons of stuff. We just take these sentences right here. They're right here. The mission of the job is to do X and Y. OK, very simple. And for that, you already have pretty much all the work done because you've got your copy sentences.

Also called result sentences well. You just use that. OK, take out the number, OK? Get rid of the number. But you take these sentences and you reformulate them slightly, starting with the mission and then and then Hagel. Hagel. You've got it. You've got that chapter here. And now onto the mission. So the mission, what it is, is basically a little bit more details, a bit more details in a bullet plan. What are they? What are these things? These are your actions. You can see how you've done all the work, really, these are your actions, sentences. There you go. OK, so nice and easy right here we are giving them. We're not wading into lots of different craziness and everything, but we keep giving them simple.

Understandable. Honest. Easy. Information. So that's when they do this and this is what kind of stuff people will do in that job. OK. Very, very simple. So they read all this. They've read all the stuff before I read this. And they see, is this for me? Is this not for me? If it's not for them. OK, we appreciate that. And they're going to leave. But if they think, hey, hey, that's nice stuff that I like to do, that's the stuff that I really, really love doing. Then they're going to do what they are going to do? They're going to keep. Keep reading, and I cannot even emphasize how people appreciate this and this, if you're being simple, if you're being honest, and by that you use simple sentences. So it's got to be simple, simple sentences straight to the point.

You don't try to reinvent the wheel or to say crazy stuff or to beat around the bush, whatever. You just say it as it is with a clear bullet point exactly what people will do. People are going to love it. People who read that sort of adverts, they convert very, very well. And they really want to work for me because they see straight away that I am not one of these recruiters who's creating something very complex that no one understands. And it's all very complicated and known. It's very simple, very straight to the point. And people appreciate that a lot. And by doing this, we keep building the interest, the key building the connection.

OK. And at the end, we have a very key sentence right here. Where do we say how? Success. He's measured. That, again, is people appreciate that a lot. They're going to say how, right? It's very clear how I'm going to be assessed. And that's also a question a lot of people have, is how am I going to assess what's going to be the KPI, what's going to be expected of me? Well, this is how you're going to be assessed. So it's very clear, priorities here, OK. And now. We've pretty much answered. All of that question. OK, we are just that thought where he is left, but I do it on purpose because I use it to seal the deal to Kevin. But all of that is done OK. All of that is done now. I'll add a little paragraph right here about the right candidates. OK.

That's the right candidate. And the idea is that, you know, when they read it. And bear in mind that nearly at the end we're here, OK? It's near the end. So I've already built a lot of interest and a lot of connections. So when they read it, they say it's me. OK. And what I use for this is simple. Attitudes. Your skill and knowledge. I just put them off here. You know, this is the sort of stuff I'm looking for and his attitude, skills and knowledge. So if you don't have any of this stuff, then don't be surprised if you don't go to the next stage, because that's what I'm looking for. And that's right here to put it there. It's going to inform. People. Then you show me. OK, show me, show me that stuff. So lots of people are very good at picking what they're going to do when they read that they're going to sing. All right.

I need to redo my CV. I need to show these things. And you know what? There's nothing wrong with that because they can do half of my job for me. I'm not going to have to go through the CD and ask myself, just have this done, whatever. No, they're going to try to make it stand out. And that's perfect, because if someone has a masters degree, that's in Book creation. I'm just giving an example of that. But they don't usually put it first, because I don't think it's relevant to what they're doing right now, because they want to like studying because they're not some cool creation from Upwork and they've been quite successful. And whenever they want to jump back into it, then they're going to put it right here.

Cool. I did a mouse inculturation. I didn't really work. And Of course, creation straight off, though, because I started working in online marketing. But I've always liked to do some cool things and I've actually had a small business on the side of Winkle's creation, and I'm going to redo my CV that just shows Gohei. That's what I want to do now. And that's perfectly fine. That's perfectly good. And that's going to help me find that right person. OK, so I always put it out there so that people know what I'm looking for. And again, it builds up, keeps doing the same thing. You know, we keep building on emotion. Interest. Because we are honest. Simple. Clear. OK.

And then after that, I put a little bit more about the benefits. I own each food that, especially if I in this one, I was looking to hire part time, so I didn't want people to come out and, you know, after all the process and say, oh, I want three thousand a month, whatever, which is normally the kind of money for for a good cause greater. But yeah, what did I do? Because I was looking for part time and it is the money I had to spend on a position. So, yeah, I put it out that you cut through other people and you can do that as well. You know, if you if you've got something very, very specific or you have a very low budget, whatever, and you know, you're not really within the right budget for that kind of role, you got some constraints wherever you can use that part as well to cut some application and be sure people to apply would actually be fully informed. OK, so that's one thing you can do most of the time. I don't actually put the salary.

I say salaries to be discussed as a competitive reverse of this. And I and I reinforce my benefits and then apply. OK, now from that's the only thing you could possibly change is you could have um. An additional apply button. Probably here. I could do another private one, and I keep rereading it, but that's basically it in terms of job adverts. OK, so you've got your chapters, you've got your objective and everything. So I'm just going to summarize it for you. Now you understand how it works. So. No one. You want to make it appealing. Number two, you want to answer the question. It's about the company that's the north you know about. What's in it for me? OK, you want to know? You want to answer what's in it for me? What kind of company and what kind of job is it? OK, that's the three key questions, OK. Number three, you want your title? You want the standard.

Job, OK, don't start putting Tetsuro, amazing opportunity. Earn whatever, blah, blah, blah. No, no, no, no, no. The title needs to be simple and needs to be straightforward. It's just got to be a nice, nice standard job name so that people know exactly what it is. Then you've got what I call the hero chapter. With the emoji. And all your nice benefits. Plus, the apply button. OK, so that's. Impress. And pull. OK. Very important. And then after that. We're going to have. Your company chapter. Then we're going to have. It was a job. With your results, sentence's. And your action sentences. Then the right candidates. That's your attitudes, skill. And knowledge.

And then. Summary of the benefits. You can talk maybe briefly about career ups. And apply. OK. That's how you structure it. All right. So do it now. Now you know how it works. You've got your do now. You create your job adverts following that model. OK, you quit your job at what point now? I will put a link in the Book. She's a PDF of that. I suggest you copy and paste out of the chapters that you have to structure straight away. And you follow exactly the structure. Yet you obviously forget about this, but mobile first. Loading time. And he keeps. Pretty cool. All right. So drink now. Great job adverts, host it on your website, whoever you want to host it, and I see you in the next chapter.

Introduction To Sourcing For IT Recruiting - How To Source Great

Hello, everyone, welcome back to this training on recruiting, I see candidates rooting for recruiting. So at this stage, it's really getting exciting because at this stage, if you remember everything we've done, we've got a gold detector. It is ready with our operating system, with our sensors. We've also got now we've worked on the persona of our applicants. We've done a lot of things. And we are pretty much ready to start sourcing, especially ours, just before we have now done our job advertising and our job advertising. You remember, we've made it very appealing. And we've made it very easy to apply in order to maximize, maximize our key metrics, really, which is view. Divided by a Soviet application, divided by view.

I got it wrong so I applied it divided by views as a percentage and saw the key metric, OK. And in order to get the views. We need you to remember we did impressions, OK? We need impressions. With only one is whoops. We need impressions now that impressions and views. That's sourcing that sort of outsourcing, sourcing applicants, finding the applicants so flashing or flashing or job advertising, you know, flashing that job ad, flashing it to as many people as we can with something that's very easy to apply and appealing to get a lot of applications. That's the name of the game right now. And the other part of it, which is now we're going to start to introduce, is, you know, it's best if they are all so early to be qualified. OK.

So we're recruiting, so we need to find people who are. Qualified in what we're doing in terms of technical roles, OK, so this is its sourcing applicant and this is the single most difficult thing to do. OK. And the problem with sourcing is that we have one major problem. Is it time consuming? And also, it's a lot of reading and reacting. OK, so a lot of hack you might find, you know, one great platform or whatever. What's working today is very different from what's going to work tomorrow. OK. Because what happens is as soon as one hack starts getting mainstream, then the people, the applicants who are on the platform start getting inflated with requests because you get more recruiters than applicants, or then the platforms start getting entry fees and so on and so forth.

So there's basically a number of elements that need to juggle. Number one is the number of active people on the platform. OK. So that's all potential applicants. Wherever we're going to flat out, we want a lot of active people. Because that gives us a lot of potential applicants, OK? The second is how qualified they are. OK. And the two go together. Then there is the competition. She's basically how many recruiters know? About that platform and use it. OK, so we want a low number. We want low competition, ideally. And then the cost, you know, the cost and ideally, you know, we want a lot of that. Right here and not much of that. OK, so that's the idea, OK.

Now, from that, you know, we have basically two ways of sourcing. OK, so we're going to study just quickly. If you get the whole logic, sourcing can go in two different directions which complement each other. But you need to be aware of that. OK. So the two directions are. No one, which is what everyone does, is finding. OK. So finding is active. OK, so that's the blue active part, OK? That's active, and that's usually either some job boards. So I go on to the job boards and I put my advert, so I'm active, I'm going out there. Or that's that's hunting, that's contacting people one by one in some places, so you can do some job hunting on some job boards, and let you contact the candidate applicants one by one.

But to me, anything that requires us to put our advert somewhere else and on a website, to me, it's active. And the key thing with this is whatever we do, that's active. It's got to fit in with our single points. Application. OK. And for that, we want the email. We've got you to email and control all of the applications into our own system. If we can't do that, then forget about it. The reason is because if you have, let's say, 10 boards. Plus a bunch of other things here that you need to manage. And every single board requires you to log on to their system and process, it's going to take forever. You know, it's an absolute killer.

So that is a big no no. One way or another, it's got to go via our own email or your own ATFs, which I'm going to talk about in a second. But if it's not possible, then you forget about this board. It's never going to work. It's going to be a complete pain and it's just going to be a disaster. So it's got to go via your email. And the other thing is that. If and this is very, very critical, if it is not. So if you can't. If you cannot get the applicants. Email. Then. It is not your application. OK, so if you can't get the email. It is not. Your applicants'. To put it bluntly, it's a bit like Amazon, you know, Amazon, if you sell on Amazon and people here who are selling Amazon, if you're selling on Amazon. You cannot get in touch with the client. It's not your client.

It's a platform for clients. So you can't get them out of the customer. You can get the address. You can get anything. OK, that's the same right here. If you go on to a job board and you're paying for using the chipboard, but they do not let you access the email of the applicants or, you know, only through the city or even in the city area, they remove it, whatever, stuff like that. That's a big no, no, we don't want to hear about this. This is not for us. OK. That means it is not your applicant. It's an applicant. And they want you to go on the platform. They want you to look, you look at you on the platform. It's going to be very difficult for you to manage. It is not right. So we avoid that as much as we can. The second way we are going to find candidates is attracting.

OK, and attracting us basically we don't lift a finger. You know, it's as simple as this. So people will. Come to us. Which is. You know, it's the ideal situation, isn't it? So we don't go on someone else's job board, we don't go and hunt whatever, we just go to put some advertising or whatever that's going to drive people either on your website or on to our Web page or whatever. We're going to see the details, but they're going to come to us through attraction message methods. So we're going to either go and find them. So that's us moving or moving a button, you know, and finding people or we going to track them.

That's a few ways, OK? Now, Of course, we always want to, you know, give precedence to this because it's the lowest effort for us. But a lot of methods right here are going to be very relevant and are going to be OK for us. OK, so that is in essence, the whole thing around saucing now from that. From that. There's different places where we can have souls. I'm going to see them together. OK, so what are we going to see in detail? I have no one. You have the list. Of balls. But I personally use and recommend a full list of boards. It's a big list, lots of countries Covid, lots of lots of boards, Covid and everything. There's a full list of boards which is included in the training, which you can go and use for that list of boards. There's going to be some trial and error, OK, for you.

You're going to have to go out there and test on board with some adverts and see the one that gives you some results, OK? Some are going to be good for some of you. Some are not going to be good for some of you and vice versa on the Internet. So you're going to have to go through a process of trial and error. But I have put a very large amount of board that I have that I know and I have used for every situation. I have also put my best boards on it. You will see I'll update that list of boards very regularly whenever I see anyone. So I'm not going to start showing you the list and this and that right now. Go on the list.

See it? It's dated regularly. It is really one of the best lists of boards, job boards right now on the markets out there that that someone is managing and updating and keeping up to date. So use that list. It is phenomenal . This is probably your best resource, OK? The number two things we're going to use for recruiting I.T. and talents is Facebook. We're going to use Facebook advertising. Facebook ads, OK, now I've got to say in the board right here, there's also going to be some Facebook and LinkedIn groups. OK. I consider them bold as well, so I'll put them in the same place so we can have some Facebook groups and also LinkedIn groups. But Facebook advertising is pretty big.

I'm going to show you exactly step by step how to set it up and how to start flashing your ads and getting a lot of applicants for it for actually very little money, even for highly technical rules. What are you going to think? Oh, no, I'm going to find some people on Facebook. Well, what did we say right here in our little study of where we're going to put our ads? Right here we said the platform. Then each has a lot of active people, which is a lot of potential applicants and ideally qualified. OK, well, if we can refine it with Facebook. If we can refine it. That little problem of people being qualified. OK, if we can refine the qualification with the audience, I'm going to show you how we get it done.

Then no one can dispute that Facebook has a lot of active people. Yeah, people are very active on Facebook, a lot of people are very, very active. Most people that are extremely active on Facebook. So it's a, it's a goldmine which is totally unexploited, which is why we really want to show it to you in a lot of details, which is why I have a full modularly. OK, number three is obviously LinkedIn. Are you going to say, oh, well, that's very expensive and nuts. Forget about it. LinkedIn is great, but there is a right way and a wrong way, and I'm going to show you the right way about LinkedIn. I think there is also a gold mine effused the proper way. But there is a right walking then, and there's a wrong way.

The wrong way is putting a lot of money and expensive ads and all that, which is not all we're going to do. I'm going to show you how to use LinkedIn. You're going to see it's a gold mine, an absolute gold mine. OK, so that's the thing then. And then after that, I'm going to put some extra stuff as well, which is going to be horses, which is going to be places from the list that I expand on. I'm going to put it in. The bonus you will see is going to be in the person that I want to be part of the whole Book. But all this I'm going to expand on some stuff. You're going to see it in the bonus. OK, so check the bonuses where they're going to be some of the stuff on it. OK. So that's what it is. That's something you don't need to do anything, actually. Oh, yes, you do.

So that you do. You don't need to do anything. So. So that's sourcing. That's how we're going to do it. OK. Now, the other thing we're finding is something that I don't have right here for you, but which you can do. Either the ideals. And you're going to say, well, that's grandchildren, but, you know, I'm not paying all these calls and everything, I thought we're going to give us everything. Yes, I can give you a lot. But there also some stuff it's going to come from you and that can be pretty powerful now. In order to add yours, there's something so simple you can do. And we have a spreadsheet. You would see our building right there just below a spreadsheet of location. What is this spreadsheet of location? So are you going to open up? So location sheets.

And in it, you're going to copy. All the attitudes. Skills. And knowledge. That she had brainstorm originally for your personal OK, so you already have all this you've done the work for all of this. So you just copy it. You just copy it on the location sheet. And then what you do is for each of these, you come up with two to three locations. Ideas. Of where you can find someone. With that attitude. Skill. On knowledge. OK, by doing this exercise, you're going to have a lot of stuff that is completely irrelevant to, you know, attitude to play. You can find someone who's a team player in the basketball team. Great. Good idea. I'll ask around your basketball club. Maybe there's someone who has the knowledge and skills you need to see.

So there's going to be a lot of stuff like this. But some stuff and especially I have found whenever I've done that work and I don't do it often enough, but I should really do it because I've often often got some great, great, great applicants and super easy jobs that are filled so quickly with that method, especially with this and this. If you know of a particular university. Maybe you've even been to this university and they are great at that knowledge. Are doing these calls, are doing these particular calls, you know, really, really good. And maybe you have a link with a professor.

Well, can the professor give his allouni? Can Professor Emeis, some of these students for an internship start working with you? Can you see you get that excuse is the same, you know that the skills, you know, like where do people learn that skill? You know, if it's a skill, for example, it is Python. OK, well, who's setting a Book on Python? Have you learned Python through an online Book? Can you get in touch with that guy? I've done it, for example, with copywriting. I've always struggled with copywriting until I've just decided to go into all the masterminds in copywriting. You know, I had a friend who wasn't a mastermind and copywriting, and he said, well, why don't you give me one of your job ads and copywriting and I'm going to send it to my mastermind.

I got great people from that. I met amazing people. So I just duplicated all of the masterminds in copywriting. And I got so many people applying. So by doing that, exacerbating that brainstorm, you're going to come up with a lot of bad ideas. OK. Like your basketball club, like this or not. But there's going to be some jam and you get you you're going to start finding some great, innovative way of finding people. OK. Now, the only thing with this is that quite often this is a little bit more mid to long term strategy. You know, it's going to take you a little bit more time to start, you know, creating a bit of a relationship with a professor here. Infiltrating the masterminds of events and that. So, you know, this is something that you, Judith, have in the background, which is why I always give you all of these things right here.

So you can get going right now, but I want you to do that exercise here, right here as well, so you can start building up recruiting strategies at the Victual term. And let's say, for example, your company is going to hire and you know, he's going to hire, I don't know a lot of python developers in the next two years. You're probably going to need, I don't know, 20, 40 of them. What I would say is get on with it right now and build some links. With all these things to start, you know, having good wine necks of python developers who can come out of uni, out of the Book, out of, you know, whatever, and yeah, just start getting that network going and really work on your location ideas and work on Fregoli, you know, add to it and add to it and keep building links because that's going to be freaky. OK, so that's what you need to do right now. You know, I would say do it now.

I'm going to do it right here. Do now. Is a complete location sheet. Go through the board lists. And start highlighting the one you want to use. And then you watch your link in your Facebook Sohi and LinkedIn training. And you implement and then you're going to be reduced outsourcing and the whole thing is going to be ready, you only need to then automate the whole thing and you already. Now, one last thing from all of this is if you have the budget for it and if you want to invest it, there are some applicant tracking systems out there that enable you to post on multiple boards in one bill. OK, which is great. Which is honestly very, very good. But the problem is that these things are usually country. Related.

You cannot do that in multiple countries, so I don't know if people are going to watch my calls and they're going to build a worldwide digital, worldwide team. Teams that are remote working and whatever. Which is why I didn't really want to touch on this, because if you are, let's say, in the U.S., you're going to be linked. You bought it in the US, which is good. That's your recruitment strategy. And then you should definitely invest in these ETFs. I don't recommend anyone. I don't recommend any of them specifically. You need to look at them and invest in them if you want to do that. So, ETFs will enable you to track your questionnaire, your test and your opinions, everything in one system.

And that's great. If, however, you want to recruit in multiple countries and have an add a team that's remote, a base and everything, then you're going to have to use my own method now in my method as well. I will actually show you how to build your own weights. Four, I'd say probably a tenth of the money. And in my opinion, having tested these things, what we are going to build is actually thought to be far superior. It is faster. It's much more flexible, easier to use. Once it's set up, it is an absolute beauty and faster, quicker, better. But, you know, I just want to be clear that there is some stuff out there that is already existing, which you can get your hands on. It's quite costly, ineffective, and very expensive.

And also, you have a lot of limitations around which balls you can use and this and that. So, you know, it's up to you to weigh the pros and cons. But I would definitely say do that and I would see you in the next chapter. 7. How to use Facebook for IT Recruiting Facebook Recruiting Starter Checklist: Facebook Page Business Manager ready Payment method added Step 1 - Add Content to Your Page A few images of colleagues and team (take Zoom screenshots) A bit of blurb on values and missions 3 posts is enough to give your page a bit of life Step 2 - Get 1000 Likes

Go on your Business Manager home page and click on "ads manager"

Click on the green
button "create"

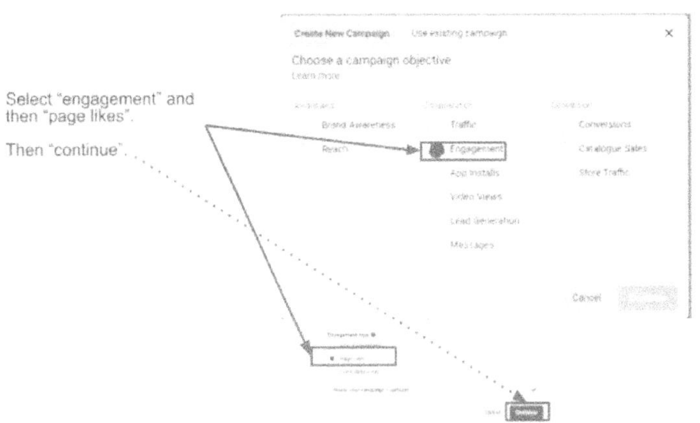

Select "engagement" and then "page likes".

Then "continue".

Give your campaign a name and then "next"

Suggested name - Like Campaign "DATE"

Give your Ad Set a name.

(An Ad Set is a groups of ads with the same parameters - Budget, Audience, Placements and Buying strategy)

Select the right page if you own more than one.

Input your budget and start date.

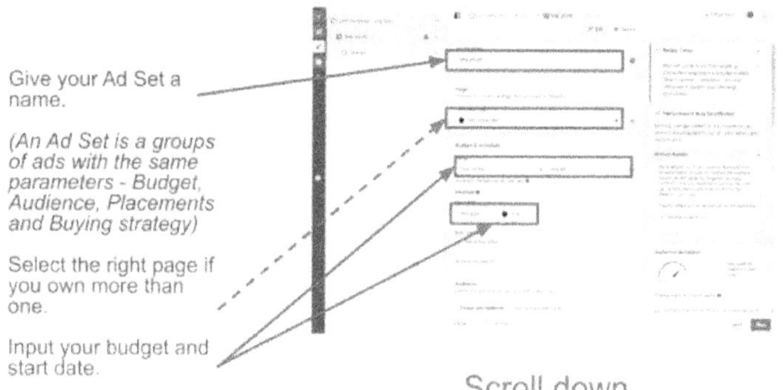

Scroll down...

Hover on "location" and click on the edit button which will appear around here

Location will appear - input "philippines" or similar country in order to get "cheap clics" (unless you want to buy expensive likes)

Scroll down the page and remove all errors if any. Leave all other parameters as is.

Clic next.

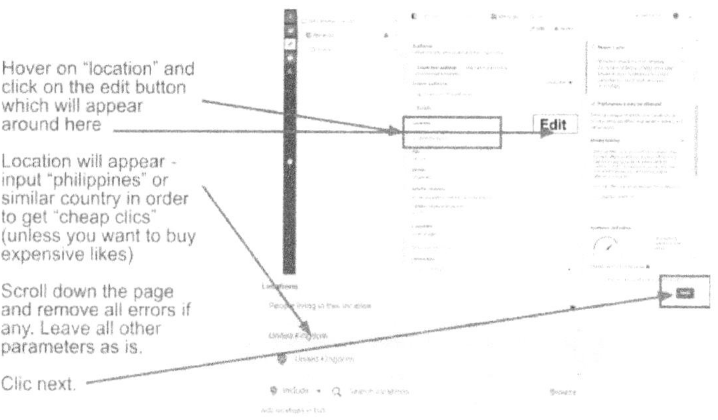

Give your Ad a name

Click Add media and
select image.

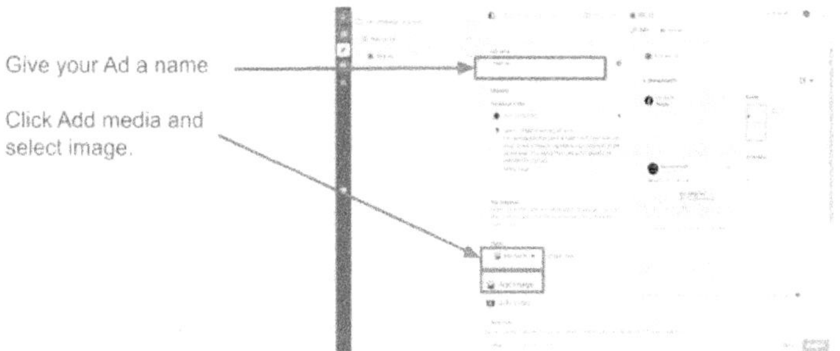

Click "upload" and
select your image from
your hard drive.

You can find free
images here and with
many competitors.

I suggest you use
either a beautiful place
image or a beautiful
young professional
woman

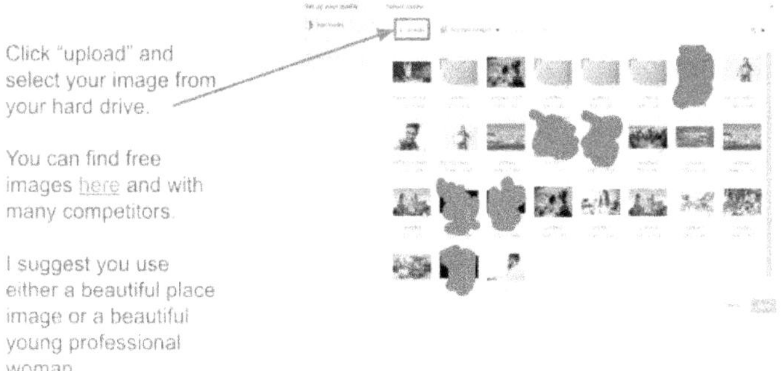

Add your text, something like "Great Job Opportunities Working From HOME -> Like Now

You can add further options as you see fit.

But with that you are good to go, click publish.

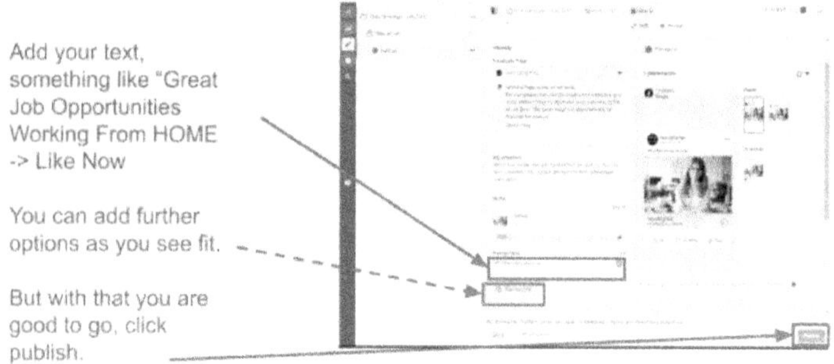

Well done - your like campaign is live

- Facebook takes a bit of time to approve your campaign, just be patient :)
- After 48 hours make sure you check your campaign results - you are aiming for a cost per like of around 0.25 cts maximum.

Step   3   -   Your   First   Recruiting   Campaign

Go on your Business Manager home page and click on "ads manager"

Click on the green
button "create"

Select "reach" and then "continue".

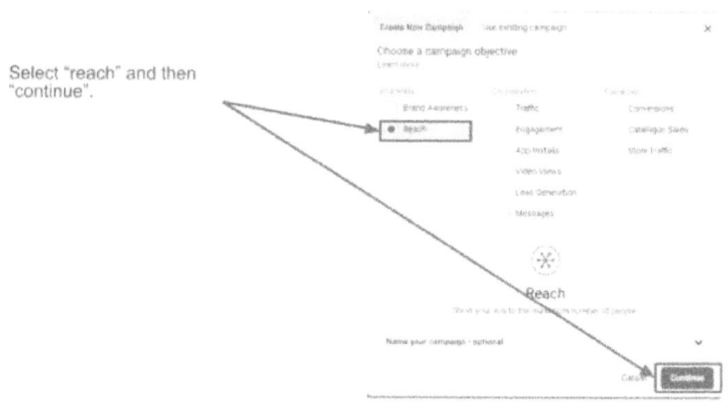

Give your campaign a name and then "next"

Suggested name - Like Campaign "DATE"

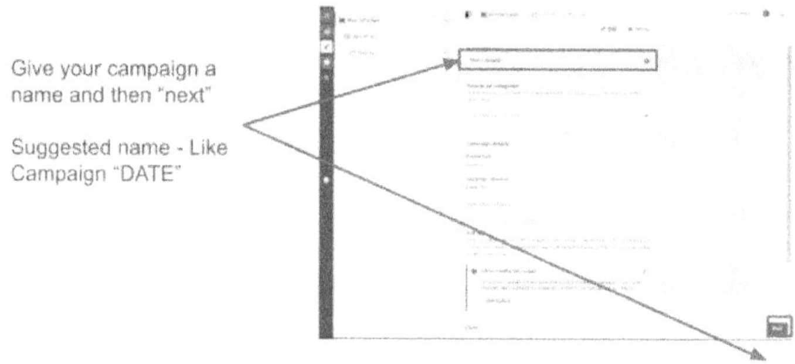

Give your Ad Set a name.

(An Ad Set is a groups of ads with the same parameters - Budget, Audience, Placements and Buying strategy)

Select the right page if you own more than one.

Input your budget and start date.

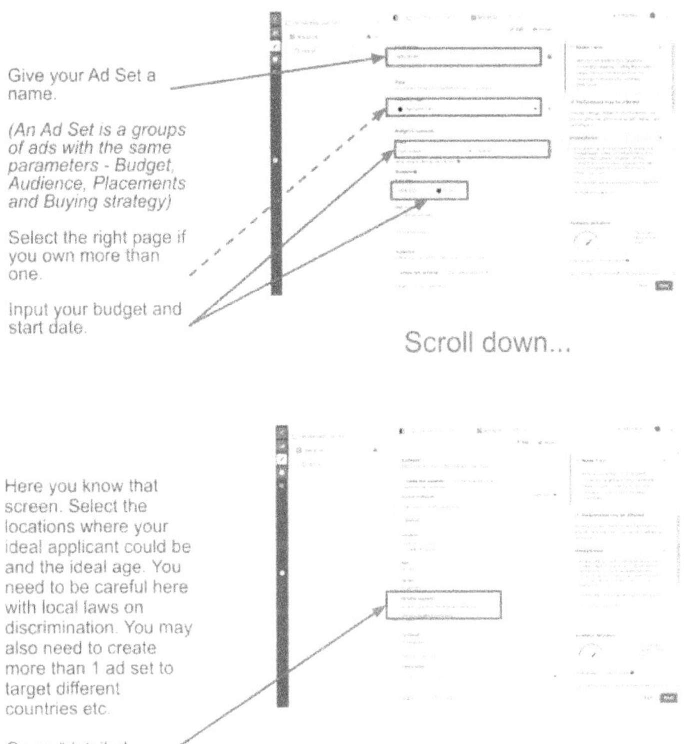

Scroll down...

Here you know that screen. Select the locations where your ideal applicant could be and the ideal age. You need to be careful here with local laws on discrimination. You may also need to create more than 1 ad set to target different countries etc.

Go on "detailed demographics"

Here you will be able to select people by interest.

What you want to do is find the right audience that will yield you "qualified applicants".

For instance if you want to recruit a Shopify Dev, you might add "shopify", "coding", "liquid", etc.

You will need to test a few things to get it right

Once it is ready go to the next steps by clicking "next"

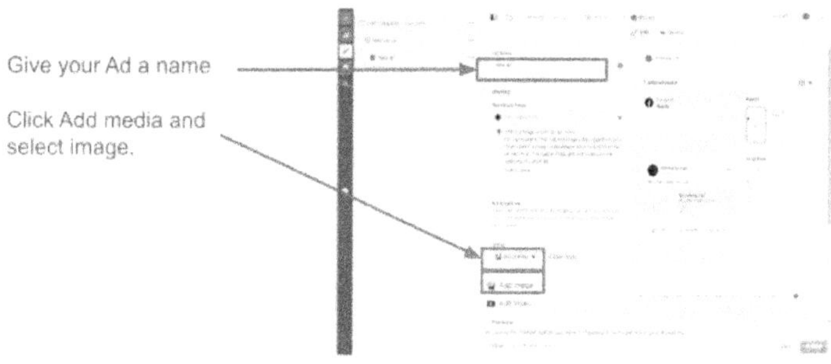

Give your Ad a name

Click Add media and select image.

Click "upload" and select your image from your hard drive.

You can find free images here and with many competitors.

I suggest you use either a beautiful place image or a beautiful young professional woman

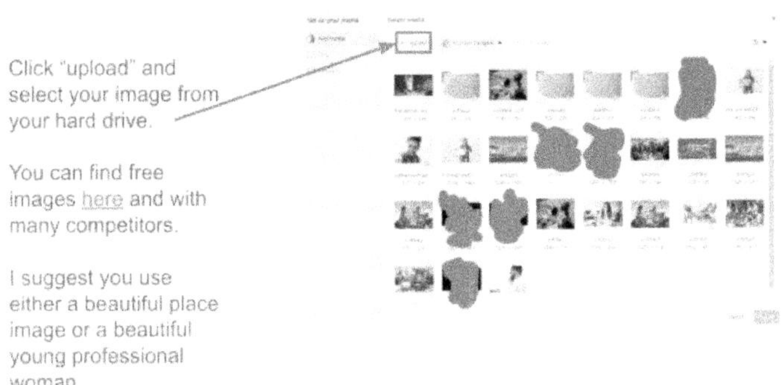

Well done - your like campaign is live

- Facebook takes a bit of time to approve your campaign, just be patient :)
- After 48 hours make sure you check your campaign results - you are aiming for a cost per like of around 0.25 cts maximum.

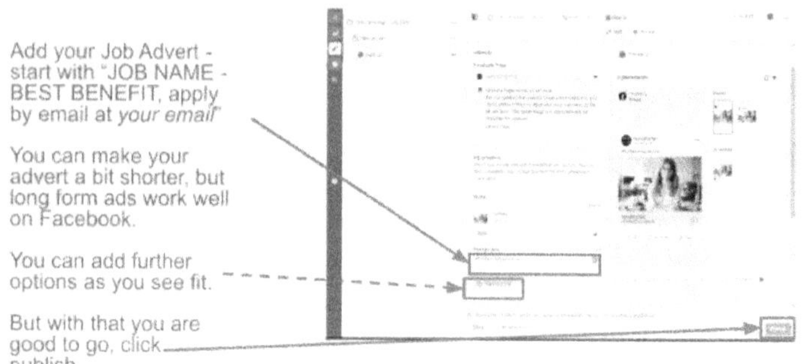

Well done - your campaign is live. Facebook takes a bit of time to approve your campaign, just be patient :) With this campaign your key result is how many emails you receive. It should cost you a maximum of 10 USD per email, and that is the most it should cost you. If you do not receive emails -> the ad is wrong, maybe the email is wrong.

How To Use Linkedin For IT Recruiting

All right, everyone, welcome to this chapter on recruiting on LinkedIn. OK, so there are a number of ways you can recruit on LinkedIn. If you have a page that is actually like what we've seen on Facebook. You can create advertising. You can do lots of different things now. I'll show you the most efficient way to recruit on LinkedIn, one that I've used for anonymous years, which is still very much funded by now and will give you a lot of good applicants. And I think it will help you fill up your jobs in record time, especially technical jobs in I.T., I.T., JOV, technical Shrove. They have jobs, that kind of stuff, but sometimes it's a little bit difficult. So here is what we are going to do.

So just. Just as we start, we are going to start with a search, going to and establish a search and that's search. Are we going to clean up what we're going to stay on or Shopify developers? So I'm just going to have a quick look before I even start on Shopify development just to see what Bing Bing is going to give me, OK? So this is how I'm going to start my recruiting on LinkedIn. OK, Shopify developer. So I. What kind of results are we getting here? I'm going to click on people. They're not going to see any results. Linden is giving me worldwide a case where one million people, according to Shopify, develop so straight away, such a title is going to be valid for me to do my search here, because right now I'm searching for people who are literally searching for people.

This is an active method. We are looking for people. We're going to hunt for people. OK, so lots of people are calling themselves Shopify developers, and that's great. I'm going to put liquid developer because liquid is a name of a language just to see just to see the difference. Let's see what this is giving us, another million results. Interesting. But you can see. People are mentioning liquids in their skills. But they don't call themselves Shopify or liquid developers, they call himself Shopify experts. So there's not as many results. And I'm seeing as well that it's mostly people who look to, you know, at first glance. Not necessarily when I leave. Interesting. All right.

I'm just going to leave it at that. And for now, let's just say I want to start contacting Joven, OK? So I'm going to find Joven and have a look at Joran and see what he says. Oh, okay. So I've got some mutual connection, which is interesting. He's a designer. So the kind of person I'm looking for. So if I want to connect and contact Joran I have to click on here and connect. OK, so I'm going to leave him a note and say something to you, Robert. Hey, I'm looking for Shopify. Expertise would be great to connect to the Senate and wait for the event to apply. And then after that, I'm going to have to manage all this conversation on my messaging. OK, so this is the low way of doing it. OK, so we're going to look at Shopify developers, liquid developers.

And you probably have done that already. You know, going to these people and listing all the complete pain is so difficult and this and that. And it is actually quite painful and difficult to do this now. That's the way we do it. The thing we're going to add is, number one, we're going to lose to look at all filters. And what we want to do is filter down to as few results as we can so that they're very, very qualified, because as you can see, this method is quite painful. So we want to narrow down a little bit. Our audience, you know, one million people is going to be pretty pretty painful to do. So one thing we can do. Number one.

So we clicked on all the filters. LinkedIn is quite painful to use, to be honest with you. So we're going to have to reload that page and get rid of Shervin, because otherwise it's going to be annoying. We're going to click on all filters. Yes. And we can never go down by location, but the most interesting thing to narrow down is to put the title here, which we see is Shopify developer. I'm going to show the results. So you see a Shopify developer who has mentioned liquid developer. We only have 1000 results. No, not interested in this anymore. I'm going to look for the word opportunities. OK. So it's going to show me people who are Shopify developers. With the word opportunity. OK.

So that means people who are open to opportunity, who have mentioned opportunities, so maybe for these people somehow opportunity is not the right word. Are we going to open? I wasn't open to new work. There you go. Open to new work. Open to new work. Again, it's not exactly what I was thinking we would get. But it's interesting, you see we are doing this in this life. So I mean, capturing some. Normally when I would open, I get other people saying, open, you're open for work, you know, open for new opportunities. That's why I also have opportunities, but I'm not getting that. So maybe that means that these people, not very many Shopify developers, actually open for new jobs, which means that it 's going to be a little bit more difficult to get them. But. Freelance.

Freelance five hundred results work. So we're getting some free answers here, which could be interesting, maybe to offer them something more stable. So you get to get the idea. So this is how we can narrow down things and then contact people who we know are freelancers or we know are open for opportunities because they have mentioned it on their profile. OK. The other thing we can filter down is obviously past experience. So if there are specific companies who, you know, gave a lot of good training on Shopify, you want to have developers who actually work for Shopify or whatever, you can do that on past companies that have competitors.

And, you know, you want to try to see their developers and you want to snatch some people potentially. You can go Covid company. Schools as well don't just want to narrow it down so you can narrow down lots of different things, language skills, that's why it's good. So all of that, you use it for narrowing down. And then what we are going to do once we have a size is interesting. I have found three freelancers. Which keywords do we have? Shopify. Developer a title, we could actually. And to get the thousand. Shopify Web designer and developer. Lead Shopify developer. So before each Wi-Fi and WordPress developer, I think it's Shopify experts. We might actually.

Covid like this are just a bit wider. OK, so what we can do once we have that is we got to keep this search and we're going to go on. There's lots of different tools which you can use. I'm going to use it because that's what I know and it always works for me. But this guy led. It doesn't really matter. Basically, it's lead generation. You can be a you want to lead generation Indian. So this is the sort of tool that people use to basically offer you their services. OK. And what is it like we expanded that enables you to basically load the search results? And then expand the will, grab all these names and search results and send them connectors, so connection requests one by one is going to send, you know, number a number of connections per day, which you can set, and then it's going to trickle down messages or first message, a second message, a third message until the reply to you.

So this is a very, very efficient way for you to actually hunt for people on LinkedIn, because all you need to reply to is the people who actually reply to your lines or messages. So you're going to say, hey, first name. So it's going to look like, hey, Erin, I'm recruiting for a Shopify developer for a company based in X. And this is what we said: would you be interested in doing it? And then if she doesn't reply, she's going to get the second message maybe 48 hours after you will set that up. Hey, Erin. You didn't see my first message. Maybe it would be good to talk about your career opportunities and then people reply to you. You know, about 50 percent of people would actually reply to you.

And then you get to start having these conversations and some of these people very quickly, you get to see like, hey, they are interested in this thing. And if you've done your work here properly on your filters, then your filters will actually have preselected a lot of the people. OK, which is great, especially because when you go like this, do you select people? It's actually a little bit harder to get them to do your test because there's a feeling that you are demanding something. So it's harder to get them to do the test.

But which you can do is if your preselection is strong enough here, you can jump on a call with them and through the call and everything, obviously you start getting them a little bit through the call, but then you say, hey, the process is this and this and this and this you role properly and then you send them to the test because you said during the call that you can there's a test to do. Right. So you vet them with the selection. You contact them with a tool automatically. And it's very, very simple, and I'm not saying use expanding, you can use any of the tools. It doesn't matter, to be honest.

They are usually around the same price, that's around 70 dollars a month, whatever. And you can use them for a month or two and then stop them. So just for your recruitment, and I would say for a very, very technical role. It's one of the best ways. It's honestly one of the best ways. And especially if you are recruiting a lot of similar roles quite often and you struggle with these roles, I would say get it now and let it run and let it run for that specific role. You always struggle to recruit because what's going to happen is that without much filtering, because what is good at what this is going to do is it's going to create you a network of people without a specific role, without having anything, nothing to do.

And if you poll regularly, especially with your profile, everything, that's going to be great. Now back on your search. So you preselect the filters, you discuss with them briefly, and then you get them on a call where you also prevent them. And in that call, you send them the opportunity and then you say to them, they're going to have to do a test, because as part of that there is a test. So make sure they're OK to do the tests on both the test and then because you've sold a role, because you've had the discussion with them. They would actually do it.

So you send them the test to get it done and then you move them to the stage or you say, hey, actually, sorry, the test was inconclusive, OK? So it's a little bit of legwork. I'm not going to lie so little bit of legwork. But with that technology, it cuts a lot of the. Yeah, a lot of the painful stuff to do, which is connecting people one by one, which you can still do, by the way, if you want to do it, you can still do it. But it is very painful. And then with the tool, you only get to talk to people about the interesting things when you say which is great. And I promise you, with that method, you will only talk to people who are actually very qualified because you've done that work here.

You're only talking to highly, highly qualified people and provided they're interested in your opportunity. Then they will usually do the test and you will obviously get a lot fewer applicants. So I would say Jews, that method in connection with Facebook and with a list to both of you. But these applicants will usually be quite high value. So, yeah, I would say use it in connection with the rest. And I think with all this method, you should be able to find great people for your jobs really, really very quickly. Actually, if you think about it, 30 days of that will yield you quite a lot of people. So that's it for this chapter. I'm not going to dwell also on these tools, especially because I don't want to promote one us, the other, whatever that expands these as Kiley's.

There's also probably if you go on this website app, Sumo, if you put LinkedIn as a search like here, they will usually have most and something we usually have something agreed on the very. You can see that you get a deal on some similar kind of work, some kind of tool. It doesn't matter which one you use. And honestly, they are very easy to set up. It's guided. It's simple. So I'm not going to like the tutorial, whatever. It's not like Facebook advertising where there's so much stuff and everything. So you can get the tool. You can do a free trial, probably have a free trial, whatever. Just get one of these tools, it doesn't matter which one. And it loads some campaigns and starts playing with them. And you will see the results are going to be very, very, very, very good for you. And that's it for me.

How To Automate Your IT Recruiting With An Applicant Tracking System

All right, so this is Meldrew, and I'm going to show you how you're going to tie everything together. So basically at that stage, you've got your job advertising, you've created your test and you created a new one. You've created all your ways where you're going to be able to advertise your job. So with all of your sourcing and now eugenics, you can get everything together in a very simple way. And the best way for that is what you call an applicant tracking system. So says a different applicant tracking system. There's lots of, I mean, lots of competitors. I'm not going to I'm not going to advertise any of them.

I would just just type the applicant tracking system and then go on them just to see a few and just get the one you prefer. It's the easiest way for you to have something that's very efficient, very, very automated, and not spend ages and ages and ages filtering manually through stuff. OK, so you want to select one that enables you to simply say yes or no to an interview and will send flows of emails and everything, basically simply choose the applicants. So just select one, just get one. And then in that tool, you would then use all everything I've shown you, you know, your job, add your test, everything in order to get as many applicants as possible and then manage them through the interview. OK.

So I'm going to keep it very simple. I have a chapter that's going to come up after and I'll put it in the bonus for this worry about how you can create your own applicant tracking system. But when I was trying to put it together, I realized it's actually quite complicated and I wouldn't want to lose everyone with this. So I think the easiest thing for you is to get an applicant tracking system, get one. A lot of them have a free version or a free trial or whatever. Just get one and you're going to be able to do something very simple very quickly with this. OK. So that's it.

Interview Management - Theory

Hello, everyone, and welcome back to this training. It's recruiting. This is it. We are now getting to the end of the training and we're getting to the interview stage, OK, so we're going to talk about the interview. I'm going to show you exactly how we're going to handle that, especially with technical people. But just as we are right here, we've done a lot of stuff together. We've created. Oops, sorry. Our gold detector. We've created a sourcing strategy. And at that stage right now, where we are, you know, the people are going to see they're going to miss you. Most of them are going to be very qualified. OK.

So I don't want anyone in this training following this Book to interview people who are completely unqualified, who we don't know whether or not they actually know the technology we're looking for. We don't know if they're going to be a fit or whatever. You know, the people that we are getting, we're going to be talking to today in this interview. There are people who are extremely qualified, you know, they've gone through our tests, have gone through all of our vetting. They are really at the end. And the interview is what I called choosing Steff. OK, so you should be interviewing, you know, around.

Depends how many rounds of interview, but I'm talking here about if it's a final interview, you know, you should be talking to four or five people maximum. And all of them should be potential choices. And, you know, the interview is to find, you know, the one. That's what the interview is here to do and should Chief, you know, so interview is not about selecting, although we still ask a few question that, you know, if there's any thing that we cannot find doing the test or if we don't do a first round interview, if we do a first round interview. The first round, if we have two rounds of interviews, a first round of interview, we do it because we have questions. That we cannot test.

And you remember the difference between questions in a test, the test they can use Google. Pretty much. All right. Questions, it's going to be enough to answer them then. So, you know, you're talking about knowledge mostly. You're talking about technical, mostly around knowledge, technical experience, stuff like that, an attitude as well somehow. But you want to be sure that if you have quite a few of these questions, you know, when you get to the interview, you have a lot of these questions. You're going to have to do a first round. You can after your first round interview, and there's nothing wrong with that.

And you can also do more, more and more now you can have something automated. Into a video interview where you put your questions and the candidates see one question and answer to the video. And so the question and he recalled his answer as a video and stuff that that's a nice one to do is, well, it's an option. But broadly, you know, your first round interview is if you still have questions that you need to test and which you cannot do a test, you know, you've got to ask questions other than this. You know, it's about choosing the applicants who are properly qualified right here. And that's all it's all about choosing. It's all about making that final decision.

All right. So that's why this interview is so special. That's why it is so. And sometimes people are very tricky to navigate. It's because they try to use a selection and the choosing at the same time, which you can't. So you want people who get to that stage. Should be very, very qualified for anyone. All of these question marks to be mostly removed. You can have one or two, but you shouldn't have a lot of technical questions and a lot of things to check at the interview stage. If you have a lot of things to check because you cannot test them, then you organize a first round interview where you're probably going to have maybe 15 people, 15, 20 people.

Which is a rock interview, which is why you have these automated stuff. I think it's OK with 15, 20 people, maybe, maybe, you know, you give that to you, you're second in command, you know. And he will find you. The four five that you know, that you get an interview with all of these questions. So I'm sorry if I repeat myself a lot here, but the interview should be with very qualified people. You know, you're talking about choosing. This is the last stage. We're not selecting any more. If there's too many question marks, then it's not going to work. You cannot choose and select at the same time. It's just going to be too much information. And your interviews are going to have to say the right place, the right atmosphere and all of that. So.

With that being said. Our objective in this interview is to choose, OK. Now. You choose. You basically have, you know, two sets of criteria. OK, the number one is, how good and everything, and that's sort of like the person is qualified, OK? But then you kind of want to assess, you know. Their potential for growth. Which is a big one. You know, can that person get to the next stage, to the next level in your organization? Is this someone going to grow or is it someone who's just going to be there for that job? OK. And you want to assess as well. With that, the motivation.

OK, so you can see we're leaving the whole like, can you use a job and whatever that's established now, I want to know, can they grow? Do they want to grow? What are their motivations? Simply because if you have if you're recruiting for to say, for example, a junior developer or a junior data analyst and you've got the senior guy who they're going to report you, who's been there for five or six years, and, you know, they're going to be there for a long time with you because there's no reason why they should leave or whatever, then you kind of want to ask yourself, you know, is this someone who's going to be happy working with him for two or three years? Or is it someone who's here for like a year and then is going to quickly win a promotion? And if that's the case, you can't get a promotion.

I take someone for a year or not somehow. And you want to be able to establish these things. But the people are not going to just just tell you these things. You can have to deduct and make some assumptions and all that. And then I'll show you how to do it. But you won't engage them with motivation and you want to gauge their potential for growth. OK, that's pretty important. The second. The second. Element of your choice is around the cultural fit. With your business, OK, so your business. It already exists. It's already got a vibe. It's already got some people working down everything. Is this person?

Is this person going to get on? With us. OK, that's a pretty important one. You know, you want to know whether or not that person is going to get on with us or not. And these adults. Whether or not the most likely to get on and probably have a bit of an issue here. OK, so that's a pretty important one. And the other one is. Do you say share? Our values and mission. And I know some people are going to think, oh, that's a bit cheesy, this, you know, like value, mission and all that, you know, they can always say yes and everything. I'm going to show you how we can actually we can actually check for that and establish, you know, among these people who is the one who share values and morals, who's going to one's going to be the most excited about what we do and all of that.

Together with their performance on your tests. Is. The choice. And at the end of this interview, you should be able to make your choice. OK, so now that we know in the interview, in the final interview what we are actually looking for. There's a few ground rules that need to, you know, operate for us to be successful at that gate. Rule number one is never. And I've already said it for the questions, but it's even more important, I never ask. Direct. Questions. So the typical one is, are you a team player? OK. That is a big no no. Because anyone who's reasonably clever is going to say yes and da da da da da da da and they're going to give you the story, OK? So what do we do with that is instead we ask questions like.

What sports or what kind of activities do you like to do? Okay, so we ask a hobby question. And we see. You know, they like to say, do you like collective sports team sport? Are they team sports? Individual sport. And then we probe, you know, what you like. Why do you like this sport? What do you like about it? And we kind of try to find out from the information. What kind of stuff they actually like, instead of asking them the question straight away like this, which is bad. We just gather information about them personally, you know, so we have some hobby questions we ask, you know, family questions, that kind of thing. We asked some previous work questions about what you liked in your previous job. What was that? What you loved? Everything. A lot of open questions.

OK, so open questions. Open questions start with why. What, how, where, when we want, you know, a lot of sorry, we want a lot of what, why and how, what, why and how, what, why and how, what, why and how. These are the critical questions. OK, and if you mix that with that, you're already onto a winner. OK, because you're going to get a lot of personal information about them and really try to understand what kind of person now this is the thing that you want to establish, what kind of person they are. So we never, ever ask direct questions. So another example with that is like if you want to ask a question, I've taught you that you want to share your values. OK, what do you think about our value? OK.

What did you think about our values? So it's great if you want to check whether or not they've read the values, but I think at this stage, if you're recruiting for highly technical people and you have the final round, you know, this isn't the sort of question you should be asking. You should be because they're going to say, I mean, if you've vetted them properly and you've got good people in front of you, so usually reasonably clever all the values are so great. They are great. I love the values. The values are so good that they are good values, OK? Instead, you want to try and see what kind of values that they have. OK, so for example, a family question is good for that.

Family questions, OK, you ask a question about the family, so what's your situation in terms of your family, what do you like to do when you're not doing work or whatever, and you see what they spend their time with? And then from these answers, you probe. And ask further questions around, so what do you value in family time, what do you value in other people? Why do you like these people instead of these people? What do you like to do? These activities and activities and the. And the thing to do as well with that, which is I'm going to use the probing number one. And then three. So three probes in your open question. Plus. Personal.

Anecdotes. So this is a really big one. So when you get to the conversation, you're asking them about their family, you start probing, you ask why you like these, why do you like that? This is interesting. Blah, blah, blah, blah, blah. You can then start. Bouncing back. With personal anecdotes, and so what you do is that you'll feed the discussions, OK, you feed the discussion. So you'll feed the discussion. And you say something about your personal life. I'm talking about your personal life, so it goes like this. You ask about the family and they say whatever family they have or have as they leave movies, a single movie that is made up this Fedotov time is our friend. Oh, that's quite an obvious thing.

Would you do with your face? Oh, we go out on a couple Checchi quite hard and everything. Oh, that's an interesting festival. No, no, I'm more like a nightclub and everything. All right, great. What you like about most of all, I like because I always meet very interesting people. So I really love meeting people. Oh, that's great. Yeah, it's interesting to meet new people and then at that stage. You bring a personal life, OK? I actually met my wife in a nightclub. If it's true or actually I met my best friend in a nightclub, I didn't expect it. And we did this. And you bring an anecdote from Elvis. OK, you tell you anecdotes and you link that anecdote. To some kind of value. And it's got to be true, you know, say something true about this, don't make it up. If you make it up, it's not going to work. But say something true.

Bring an anecdote that's going to link about some of your values, you know, personal value. You don't need to make it about the company, the company values our sustainability and honesty and whatever, blah, blah, blah, blah, blah. Just talk about your own values. Just talk about your own values. You know, I met that guy and we started really getting on because, you know, it was really fun. And we started doing fun things. And I was saying I have a lot of time for him, and he's my best man at my wedding because I think, you know, he's got, you know, great honesty or great judgment. And I can rely on him.

And I think it's very important to be around people and everything. And then you go about like, what do you think about that? And you see what they say. And usually what happened is that because you are talking about personal life, you're bringing something personal. People will match. That behavior and that's what we want. OK. That is what we want. That is so important. So you talk about your personal life and you see that people are going to match you. And they're going to open up. And they're going to talk about it. Their personal life. As well and their own values. They're going to tell you what's important for them. Many people, when they do an interview, they think it's only the person who is being interviewed, who is being interviewed, who's got to give. OK, so they are sort of like.

Close position. And they ask questions. And sometimes even worse, a right answer. That's because they're getting confused. So. That's because they're getting confused, like I explained at the beginning, if they are selecting. We don't do that. We are choosing. And if you want to choose properly, you've got to have a discussion. It's got to be a discussion and you need to be on an equal footing. That is so critical. You've got to be on an equal foot, you've got to be equals, you've got to be talking equal to equal. And it's got to be a discussion. And you're not there to just, you know, treat them with some funny question and whatever and then the answer and see if they go to work. That's not the point at this stage. The point is for you to choose.

And if you don't choose, you've got to have a discussion. And if you want a discussion, you want to know you want to get deep into what kind of person they really are and whether you can actually get on with them and everything. And for that, you've got to give something away and you're going to have to start talking about your personal life. You've got to bring anecdotes, talk about your values as well, say why things are important and say if you had a crisis at some point and you left the job, whatever, talk about these stories, because then people are going to match. People are going to match, OK, and they are going to open up as well.

And they're going to give you a lot more about their personal life and their values. And this is how you start to see whether or not they are compatible, because to be honest, anyone can say, well, my values of that, anyone can say if they read your website, that they are a good fit. I am a good fit. Well, that's not so good, you say, that's for me, too. C. If you are. And for that, I need to start to get to know you. And the question is not whether or not they already share these values, they already share the mission, everything is whether or not they are compatible. OK. That's the key one, that's compatibility in their own brain program.

Are they compatible with what we are trying to do and achieve from this mission and value standpoint, are they compatible with what kind of people we are, the. You know, as a team, or is this just going to be a complete disaster because they're not going to understand us and are going to be excited about what we do and it's just not going to work, OK? That's what we're looking for. If they're compatible, then by being with us and everything, they're going to start adhering to our values and embracing them and everything, and some people are going to be more enthusiastic than others, and it doesn't really matter.

The point is compatibility. OK, and we are looking for one. Number five is. Excitement. Are they going to enjoy it? Are they going to enjoy working with us and are we? Going to enjoy working with him. OK. And so for that, we're going to use our personal anecdotes that have been said and we're going to use very open questions that are never, never, never direct to and. Yeah. Number six is. It's a discussion. And we are asking innocuous questions. We are getting to know each other. We are asking questions around our life, around who we are as a person, what kind of life event we've had. We're going to change some anecdotes and a bit of fun, a bit of banter.

It's going to be fun and everything. But the point is that through this, we're getting a lot more information that we would ever have than we would ever have. So. It should feel. As if. We are having a chat. That's how you should feel, as if we're having a chat and it is your job. And I'm going to put it here as No.7. It is your job. To lighten. The mood. It is your job to control the atmosphere and the discussion and make the personal interview very, very, very comfortable. OK, so I would say it is pretty important. That's it. From the beginning. You lighten the mood from the beginning. I would say a half with an anecdote ready to talk about the company in some funny way.

Make just just bring a story about the meeting that's just finished and someone did something funny or whatever. Doesn't matter. But from the beginning, you need to bring a very casual, very relaxed, very light atmosphere to the discussion. Even if it's some room, even if they come to your office, whatever, you have to bring that very light touch, that very relaxed way to make Johal that person really open up and really relax. And this is how you're going to get a lot of information about them. So it is so critical that you don't just jump with a big gun and start asking questions about whether that employer, which was the last job and it's not you, doesn't do that to you straight away.

You come in, you introduce yourself, you ask where they're from. You make a few jokes and you take a good five long minutes to talk about some anecdotes, talk about some stuff that you were doing before. How big of a laugh and everything. And then only you just say so. Tell me a bit, what have you been doing in the last two or three years? Just rephrase that, have a bit of an idea, and then you get the discussion going with that and you gauge that discussion around personal stuff. You want to know about personal stuff. So all of your questions need to be open, questions that are not. Interview type questions about team players and stuff like that, but general questions about their life and you want to paint the picture.

What kind of person now that is so important because that's what's going to enable you to really choose between people who are most often more or less the same in your test. OK? So that's the interview. That's what I have for you. You will also get the sheet, because this model is right here. I appreciate it is a little bit maybe vague, but on purpose if you get a feel for what we're trying to achieve. I also put a sheet to recap exactly, you know, the steps of the interview and how you can go about it. So now we look clearer. But I really want you to give me that content. You know, take 10, take 20, 30 minutes to really give you that content about how we handle you.

And the key things around, making it very personal, having personal questions, having a chat discussion, being an equal and everything to really enable the person you interview to, you know, be relaxed and give you a lot about who they are as a person, because that's what is going to enable you to make a decision. And at this stage where you're at. This is the last piece that you're missing. You know, you've tested them professionally. You've Tetsuya's skills and attitudes and knowledge and all that. Now you need to get under the skin of who they are as a person to, you know, find out whether they're compatible with you in terms of their motivation, what they want to achieve and all that. OK, so take the sheet.

I want to have you give you that big theoretical background here. But then from a practical standpoint, there is going to be a cheat sheet that you're going to be able to use and manage the interview with. OK. Thank you very much. And go and take the sheets. And then we got you all set up for your interviews. 11. Interview for IT Recruiting - Cheat Sheet Interview Cheat Sheet Key Rules - No direct "interview" questions -> OPEN PERSONAL QUESTIONS Lighten the mood and make them feel relaxed -> SHARE PERSONAL STORIES You want to know them as a PERSON, you are here to CHOOSE not to select The key is their motivation and their values - Start of the interview - Introduce yourself and thank them for their time Ask.

where they came from / where they are taking the call from, share where you came from today / where you are taking the call from Have something funny to say - if nothing else just use the weather and talk about a problem you had one day with the weather, something light and quick -> you want to start by giving away something personal You can also use sport, last time you visited where they are from, etc Once that is done explain the process - we are going to have a chat, you will talk to me about who you are, where you are professionally, and I will talk to you about the company, and at the end there will either be a match or no match.

If there is a match we will make you an offer, and if there is no match we will be honest about it and there will be no hard feelings either way. Whatever the outcome, I want you to have the opportunity to ask all the questions you want and get a very clear idea about the opportunity we are potentially offering you and about our company and who we are as people. Sounds great to you? I suggest you literally use this script to transition to the actual interview part, because that script here works very well. Middle of the interview - You want to explore the following topics: Hobbies - this is a goldmine Family - their own family but also brothers and sisters, how they grew up School and Uni, what kind of student they were First job and career - what kind of employee they are.

Here you do not want to ask direct job questions, you want to explore what they liked in the company, why they joined and why they left What they want to do - you want to understand professionally and also personally what stage they are in their life and if it all fits together All throughout this process you want to make this a discussion and give out a lot of information about yourself as well, on the same topics. Make you prepare these as well. Once you have all the info you need, offer to ask them questions about the company. Let them ask any questions they want, keep note of the questions they ask. This will give you indication on what matters to them. Once they are done you can finish the interview by explaining the decision-making process and when they can expect to hear from you.

Step 1: Believe in Yourself

Being successful is as much about self-confidence as anything else. People who constantly doubt themselves often can now reach their goals because they are an active source, acting like saboteurs, preventing them from doing the things they want to do. That's why the first step of success and mindset is believing in yourself, dealing with naysayers and self -doubt. Would you set a goal? You might find that people in your life express dolls and dismiss your goal as unreasonable or unattainable. You may also hear a little voice in your head that says you cannot do what you want to do. If you want to succeed, you have got to find a way to silence both the naysayers in your life and your negative inner critic.

Listening to these are some of the gate your best efforts and ensure you don't achieve success with the naysayers. You've got three options. Ignore them and let the negativity roll off your back, talk to them and wisdom not to be negative straight away that are a company. The right tries to vary from person to person. Sometimes friends and family don't realize that they are being next to you when that's the case. A simple hey, I really appreciate it. If you find a way to be positive about my goals might do the trick. Some people might be unwilling or unable to curb their negativity. When that's the case, you have to decide if you can't ignore it or if you're better off letting their company choose the option.

That's right for you. Awaiting the inner critic is more challenging because you carry it around with you. A good option is to reframe that negativity. And they may imagine that instead of talking to yourself, you are talking to a dear friend. You wouldn't be rude or incite Citytv to a friend. So don't treat yourself that way either. Identifying your strengths, believing in yourself, is easier when you recognize your strengths. You Augustines we do well, so why not celebrate so you can cultivate a mindset of self belief by making a list of the things that you do best and you agree to salesperson in the waiters, a team builder right now, your strongest traits and abilities, and then turns them into affirmations when you are huling into a meeting or negotiation or planning session list and remind yourself that you're a terrific, terrific negotiator and a strong speaker.

I'll put a spring in your step and help you maintain a positive outlook. Overcoming fears and negatives . The flip side of knowledge. Your strengths are looking at your fears and negativity, negative thoughts and finding ways to overcome them. We were all afraid of something which sets us apart is how we handle those fears with negative thoughts. Try reframing them as things you would say to a friend. You can even write out your negative thoughts and then write them with a positive spin. Fears are a little trickier. You're going to need to face them. Look for ways to give yourself that too. You need to overcome your fears. For example, someone with a fear of public speaking, my the Toastmaster to get critique and encouragement from fellow members building a business plan.

Sometimes people fail due to a lack of planning. You have a better chance of achieving your goal if you are concrete, the plan for achieving them. Writing a business plan takes time and effort. You will need to think about your specific goals and break them down into actionable steps, decide what resources you will need and how you plan together and the immediate and short term long term goals. The benefit of writing a business plan is that it will help you clarify your goals. Make it easier to tell if you got a goal that is too ambitious or not ambitious enough. How people fine tune your ideas serve as a template for approaching investors, partners and others to talk about your business.

It might be a lot of work, but the time you spent on your business plan will help you achieve a successful mindset. Getting inspiration from successful people when you are aiming for a lofty goal is easy. To get discouraged is also easy to look at other successful people and tell yourself you cannot do what they did or that they were never you. The truth is, everybody struggles in some way. You can find inspiration by seeking out stories about success. People who overcame negative thinking or other obstacles. One example is the noblest of Stefan King, one of his earliest known Kerry was rejected by more than 30 publishers before it was finally accepted.

If he had given up, he wouldn't be one of the most famous and successful authors in the world. Did you know that Bill Gates had a failed company before he started Microsoft? And that was Walt Disney fired by the Kansas City Star because his editor said he lacked the imagination and had no good ideas. The point here is that if you let the naysayer hold you back, you won't be successful. The only way to succeed is to believe in yourself, then take care of step one. In the next chapter, we will talk about how to test your ideas. Keep reading this chapter to learn more.

Step 2: Testing Ideas to Prove Them Worthy

You probably have tons of ideas, some are good and let's face it, some are not all. Can you tell the difference that testing them with testing ideas and products is important? Testing your ideas and products is essential. It's not that hard to understand why. Which would you rather do? Spend your time and the money developing and launching a product only to find out that it doesn't sell that way? You saw it would some time. Testing and the refining aren't there first unless you're hard earned dollars in launching it. The answer is clear, right is better. Use your time to test that thing out first. Once you have tested and refined your idea and the retest, you will have plenty of good ideas of whether it's going to work. Market research.

One way to improve your chances of success is to do market research before you spend valuable time and money trying to start your business. So I mean, pitching your idea to a few valued friends or family members and might even mean asking your blog readers what they think of it with the product. It's a little trickier, but you might do a Google search for products in your niche and spend a few minutes on Amazon seeing what's available. If there is a product that does exactly what yours will do, you will need to reconceptualize. The most important thing with a testing idea is to make sure you have got a unique value proposition. That's the one seeing your product or idea that nobody else has.

Your value proposition could be about functionality or it could be about price. The main thing is to know how you will differentiate, differentiate your product from others on the market, identifying the problems and finding the solutions. You're more likely to succeed if you identify a product or service that provides a solution to our problem faced by your target audience. People go online to find answers. They ask questions and look for products that will help them. You can find problems by searching a common keyword in your niche and looking at Google search. See the searches, for example. Say you want to create a product in the patronage and then you go looking for it and go for a puppy training product. You might search how to house, train a puppy and see something like a list of the other suggestions.

You can see there are some ideas there, including focusing on training with a bell or training with the crate. You might be able to carry out a niche for yourself by focusing a training message for people who work during the day. That's a problem that might now be addressed by other products. And that means you could be your unique value proposition, setting goals and the small steps to success. Do you know how to set goals even more, saying I want a successful business? You might have heard about a smart cost. It means setting goals that are specific, measurable, attainable, reasonable and timely. This Book is about a success mindset, but success isn't a specific enough word when you are setting goals. Here are some examples of smart goals. Incorporate a new business.

Generally, the fifty thousand in revenue in the first year attracts ten new clients in the first quarter. What you will notice is that these goals are all specific and achievable and in the case of the revenue and client base, the goals are measurable and timely too. When you set goals as if they are smart and if they're not fun to them and they are planning for failure, you are probably thinking it's strange to plan for failure. It does, but it's also a smart thing to do. Everybody remembered the story about the seven Kings being rejected thirty times by publishers.

The reason he is a beloved and highly successful author we know today is because what he did after those rejections, he didn't stop. He didn't give up. He learned to cope with a rejection and he persisted. Before you start, Ozalp you will do. If you fail, keep asking and plan for it. Understand that you may fail and know that you are still in the game unless you take yourself out of it. Coming up next, we will talk about the next step, which is related to failure. So few people learn from their mistakes and you all learn how you can.

Step 3: Learning from Mistakes

Every cloud has a silver lining and the soul makes every mistake, it's a big cliche to say that mistake, a learning opportunity, but a fact that is a common saying doesn't make it untrue, just like a failure. Mistakes show us who we are. We all make them. It's what you do with them that marks the difference between success and failure. Why does starting off fail? It's not easy to get a star off of the ground when start ups fail. It can be for any of several reasons. Here are some of the best comments. No one is not focusing on customers and solving our problems. Number two, lack of focus, the necessary scaling too quickly. Number three. Number four, not building a successful team. We have already talked about focusing on customers.

If you do that, you will be halfway to success because you won't be thinking about yourself. You'll be thinking about your audience. Focus problems have when you try to do too many things at once, simplifying goals and focusing on one product or idea will help keep your eyes on the prize. Scaling is something that can send an entrepreneur into a tailspin. Allow your business to grow organically and the scale only when you are ready. We have to talk about how to build a successful team later. But suffice to say you cannot do everything yourself. Reframing mistakes as opportunities. Nobody likes making mistakes. It is no fun to be wrong. But every successful entrepreneur needs to get comfortable with it and learn to see mistakes as opportunities.

What happens when you mess up? If you pay attention, you can learn something. Everything you learn now will help you with your next goal. When you make a mistake, take a deep breath and ask what I learn from this. And then once you have identified, use a chapter to grade your next opportunity. Once you get in the habit of doing it, it will be easy to reach your goals. We already talk about small goals. When you don't achieve a goal, it's easy to feel disheartened. Often it is just a sign that your goal was way too big. If you are ever made a to do list, you may have noticed how gratifying it is to cross all the items on it.

Some people even post similar things on their list because they know they will be able to complete them quickly. When you set goals for yourself, take every long term goal and to break it down into the smallest possible steps, focus on what you want and narrow goals to help you achieve. You'll be far more likely to get where you want to go if you have tight, achievable goals. How do you vandalize the experience? Everything you experience is a chapter. When you make a mistake or fail, it's natural to be upset, take time to be upset, but then setbacks. That's what you did wrong and what you would do differently next time.

If you lack information, go Funday, read, study, talk to other people in your industry and then talk about what you take, what you have learned to heart and then use it in the future. Testing. While the best way to refine your goals then have fun with your product is with split speed. Testing involves mostly taking content on an ad campaign and testing different words until you get the best results. So the key to split testing is testing only one element at a time. Not satisfied with your face will ask for two different highlights.

Choosing that one performs the better and the split test you'll call to action creating your plan B. It's always a good idea to have a plan B if your first idea doesn't work or you will try next. There's no shame in having a backup plan. In fact, part of the reason that successful people become successful is that they have a backup plan. Coming up next, we will talk about how to keep focus on your customers so you don't get off the track. Keep reading to learn more.

Step 4: Focus on Your Customers

The customer is always right. That's a true sense of customer service, but it's just as important that when planning for success in the last chapter, you will learn that the one of the main reasons to fail is because they fail to focus on the customer or you're not going to make the same mistake. Why you should focus on what customers want or need. Your customers are the lifeblood of your business. If your kids are not happy, your business will fail. It's that simple. We have already talked about market research and testing. Even after you have a test of everything, though, you still need to focus on your customers. It doesn't matter what critics of your company or product say.

If your customers are happy and satisfied, you only make money. Sing about James James Carville's famous son during Bill Clinton's presidential campaign. It is the economy, stupid. It was a reminder that Campins Water customers will worry about the economy. Keeping their focus on the community helped make the campaign a winning one, creating a great start to finish when a customer's experience with you starts when they first learned about Conley or Foda or continues for as long as they use a product. When you think about a customer experience, every step of the experience offers stellar content and an easy buying process.

And Asselin support customers who have achieved a top notch support are remembered due to their friends providing value. What is the secret to attracting customers' value? Before anyone spends their money on your product, they are going to want to know they will deliver on its promise. You can make them feel better about that by offering clear value to them even before the Barthe buy. This means that creating and delivering interesting, informative, relevant and actionable content, they will help you engage their attention. Delivering value triggers a mental glitch called reciprocity. When you give customers something for free, even its information they are more likely to feel obligated to buy from you.

Of course, while you must confront your product as well, the quality of the product is useful in its long activity and its price becomes authority. People look up to authority figures. You can prove your authority by doing what you just talk about delivering value to your customers. But our society is more than that. It's about showing that you are a reliable and knowledgeable resource of information on social media and delivering original content that is informative and actionable. It may also mean curating content in the industry publication A.R.T. and then sharing it with your own take on the topic. One way to establish yourself as an authority is to offer a lead into Grolier.

Least leading can be a Schrieber, a tip sheet, a template or anything else that demonstrates your knowledge. Customer support, customer support staff. When a customer first visits your website, they usually sing about what kind of support your customer needs and how you were delivering on the day. Support will most likely in person and on the phone today you may want to sing about email support Chata Support Shadbolt Self-service Options, FNQ Social Media Support. You will need to test the various options to figure out what will work for your audience. Remember that a lot of companies are merging social media with support and consider doing the same. Now we will talk about the fifth and the final step to success building a successful team.

Step 5: Building Your Success Team

If you want to be successful, you cannot go alone. There's a temptation to do that. Of course, we're doing everything possible that may save you a little money, but in the end, it will cost you more in time and sanity than the alternative. Why? You shouldn't try to do everything. You might have a lot of skills, perhaps, that you are a great innovator with excellent communication skills. Maybe you're dabbling in accounting and flirting with marketing. No matter how good you are, you are not food and everything. If you try to do the things you are not so great about, you might wind up settling for less than perfect results.

A lot of entrepreneurs do everything at first you might need to, but once you have established your business and products, it's a good idea to branch out and get some help. Not only will you be able to do a better job at the things that only you can do, you will also be able to live a balanced and productive life. And that's part of the success heaps of building a team. The idea of building a team can be an intimidating one, particularly if you are thinking about and you need to hire people and deal with taxes and insurance. The good news is that you don't need to do those things unless you want to.

Lots of companies outsource taxes as needed and without hiring full time or even part time people, the first step is to decide who you need for your team. Are you struggling to keep up with social media? You may also want to outsource it to someone with more experience. Perhaps you need a bookkeeper to come in once a week to pay bills. Maybe you need a payroll service. You might decide to hire someone full time. Keep in mind that there are plenty of tasks that you can't outsource to freelancers. Using sites like artwork make it easy to fund the work. Your assistant and team templates, team members, the importance of dedication.

How do you know what to do yourself and what to delegate? That education is an essential skill. You know, you can't do everything. They can be difficult to let go of things you have a customer accustomed to doing even when you have help. Here are some questions to help you learn how to delegate and for each task and teach someone else to do it. Is there anything that I'm unable to teach? Is my personal input required? Do I have someone in my team who is capable of learning how to do it? Unless that has absolutely required your input and the skills, it should be open to delegation.

Yes, you will need to spend some time training your staff or freelancers to do the tasks to your standards, you're private enough, fielding a few questions and possibly correcting a few mistakes. There's nothing wrong with keeping ketosis to yourself or your goal should be to maximize efficiency while also prioritizing accuracy. It can also be helpful to take an inventory of your team skills that might have abilities you don't know about yet.

Final Words

Thank you for taking this successful month's Book, the five sites outlined here are the ones you can use to travel the road to success. Keep in mind that you will need to, number one, reframe Nagati resources and talk to yourself as you would to a friend. Or why didn't you people and naysayers test your ideas throughout L.A. before launching your new products? Prepare for failure and learn from your mistakes whenever possible and stay focused on your customers and their needs and get the help you need to return calls. A lot of success is believing in yourself and getting the support of both yourself and others to reach your goals. If you can maintain a positive mindset and be myself while planning, then you will have the success you deserve. Best of luck. And here is to your success.

Continue learning with Weekly Case Studies

Congratulations on finishing this Book. However, this is only the beginning, not the end. The next stop, you will have to apply what you have learned in this Book to the real world. You might feel a little scared initially, ready to dive into the real business world all along. But do not worry about that. I'm here for you. The next chapter of this Book is a continuation series of weekly business case studies. So every week I will send you one new educational chapter of a real world business case study. In this study, I will show you exactly how I came out with this business idea. It could be entrepreneurship or it could be investing. Right. And step by step, details on how I put them into practice.

And finally, I will show you the real world result, what kind of business revenue will be achieved, what kind of business we made so that you don't have to repeat it right. And you can learn from that and understand how this business idea works. So stay tuned to our weekly case study. And if you have any questions, I will go online to do a live QA to explain to you and interact with you to help you succeed in your business and in your investing projects. I'm hearing down here, I sincerely hope you like this Book and also join us in the weekly case study. I will be connecting you through your journey of this learning and starting your own business, and I hope you become successful in every aspect of your life. So thank you so much for taking this Book. I will see you in the next weekly case studies.

Recap

Hello and congratulations on finishing your success Book in this bonus chapter. I want to share with you my first hand experience and a case study that you can learn from my own experience of how I came from zero to hero and to achieve success based on the mindset I learned in my life. And I teach in this Book that you can definitely grow and learn from that. Right. So first of all, I believe that everyone has the potential to achieve anything they ever wanted in their life. When you feel down or being in a losing turn and you don't believe in yourself, you start to believe that, oh, I deserve to live a life like this. I do not deserve to achieve anything I dream about. I do not desire to achieve anything in my goal that you are totally wrong. I'm not just saying that this is nonsense.

This is just saying that I want to put it into practice, that everything people grow into from zero to hero people grow based on their observation of their word and how they make the right decisions. If you have the desire really, really hard, you want to be successful. You really want to make that money. You want to start that relationship. You want to be the person who is famous for your expertise. You definitely can do it. It's only a matter that you don't want is so hard. If you want it really hard, you dream about it, you sing about it, you leave and the breeze will be that you will definitely get there. You will sink up every possible solution that you can ever think about. You just think about it.

Every person that you can connect with who can help you, you will do everything to improve your skill and your talent so that you can achieve the goal and the position you want to be. Right. So they all start from the mindset, you know, mindset is self does now help you to actually get a thing done. Right. But it's like an engine in a car. It helps you to actually put yourself in the right shape or the right position to actually formulate a strategy and the process to actually do it right. You have to put into work, put into action, and you have to do things that are required to achieve success. But if you do not have the dream, you do have to have the goal.

You do not have that strong desire to believe and the wall to achieve those success. You are achieving nothing. You're just hanging there like everybody else. Right, who don't give a lot of attention to their life, who just live every day by day, you know, without any dream or like goal. Don't do that. If you're young, you have a lot of potential to achieve in your life. And even if you were getting to your middle age, you still have a lot of things to do or to improve your life to the point of not giving out any hope and always having the mindset to learn and believe in your tree. And starting from there, your body and your life will start working on itself. Right. And then say, well, do the work to actually achieve anything in our life. You will. As I said, you won't do the same planning starting from funny.

You will do the planning to step aside to achieve your goal. You will actually connect with the people who help you to achieve your dream, to give you the shot that gives you the opportunity to actually show your talent, to show your skills or show your product or services. You definitely can do it if you want it so hard. What if you do not want it so hard to know what your goal is, right? That comes back to your experience. Life experience, you can say, but don't be too rushy. You can spend some time to experience different things in your life and then find out what you really feel passionate about and stick to that goal and the goal that passed firmly and consistently in the Ljubo to get there. A few years ago, I was at the bottom of my life as well.

There were several setbacks in my life. Almost everything I wanted to do was a failure at that time. And I know very little about the business. I know very little about confidence or self-esteem. I do not know anybody to teach me or show me how to become successful in my life other than starting from there. I was lucky that there were a few people who helped me to teach me why you give me the insight that what is the right thing to do. And the most important thing is they actually made me believe again, you know, even though you might think it is impossible to change yourself and come back if you are at the rock bottom of your life. Right.

But is there someone or some people who teach or share their knowledge to make you believe that you can actually achieve those things in your life? You can come back, you can change your life. You deserve a better life in your life that you don't want to, you know, just leave every day like everybody else or just stay at your rock bottom. Never come back. No, you can refuse to do that. So I had a person who could teach me and show me how to do that. And I tried to follow his footsteps. And gradually starting from there, I start to see myself improving every single day and most of the time, even one direction. Did you give you the right clearway? Right. Did you give the reward? You want children on her way to fund another fun. Another possibility, right.

You are very versatile. You have a lot of possibilities. You can definitely define and explore different things in your life and finally achieve your goal. You're automatically you start from the very beginning. Right. The point is, you definitely need to believe in yourself, use a mindset of power to change your life. And no matter how difficult you are, I know life goes into a lot of difficult situations, no matter how difficult you are like I was a few years ago. You my rock bottom never give up, never give up hope. And starting from the start to the fun, were you going to be where you want to be and the plan for that flower career, possibly a few milestones.

And what this is what you need to do to actually step one step, two steps, three achievable goals and to work on different milestones to give you a concrete action, to give concrete steps, concrete tasks to yourself that this is what you want to do. Right, using your precious time, using your social network connections and using the skill and knowledge you already know and using your own body that you're born with and also the talents and the gifts you have, you should put them into good practice. You can definitely achieve your goal. I can do that. You can do that, too. And I believe you have the potential to achieve anything, you know, and if you ever want it, I hope you can learn from this and that you can definitely become successful in your life and actually achieve anything in your life. Thank you for taking this Book, I'll see you next time.

Beginner Steps To Get Organized & Manage Time Effectively

Hello, I'm excited to see you. Please accept my warm welcome and let's dive right in to look at a quick overview of what you can expect to find in the Book. I highly recommend you start by downloading the Book syllabus attached, this document will guide you throughout the Book and you can use it as a checklist to keep you on track with your progress. The main aim of the Book is to provide a simple yet very effective practical strategy so that students can prioritize effectively and learn how to manage time with their energy levels. This Book also boosts productivity and results in getting more confident when prioritizing different types of tasks and workload. chapter one gets you started with the Book. Chapter two covers important fundamentals that prepare you to prioritize effectively.

You will learn three different criterias of how to get prepared to prioritize effectively, you will learn how to prioritize and perform a PDM scan in chapter three, you will learn three different methods of prioritizing. And chapter four covers one of the main contexts of this Book, which is the prioritization process, workflow. After completing the first four chapters of the Book, you will be ready to perform the steps in the process and chapter five covers the last major context of the Book, which is to manage time effectively with ETC and energy levels. Thank you for reading this Book. Let's get started.

Importance Of Prioritization

Now that you downloaded the Book syllabus, we are ready to start. This chapter is all about preparation. We will take a close look at three components that will help you in further stages of the Book. You will learn the importance of prioritization, why we really need to categorize and how to implement a PDM Scan. If you have any questions, feel free to check out the Q&A chapter below. In this chapter, we will look at why we really need to prioritize by covering two main approaches that enable you to prioritize your workload effectively. Do you ever feel like you are doing a thousand things but not getting anywhere? Well, the first main approach clearly eliminates this problem.

It is called the VYT Approach, which is an acronym for the words Valuing Your Tasks. We all have our own unique areas of responsibilities, and when starting our day at work, everybody intends to be as productive as possible. At many times we start working on tasks as immediately as they get our attention. This might seem correct, especially when we have a lot of things to do and all might seem urgent. You might be saying to yourself that completing minor and easy tasks first will give room for the important things to do. Unfortunately, this is only a great way to procrastinate from actually doing the important things. This is why valuing your tasks approach is important.

It simply gets you to question your tasks before you start executing them so that you don't find yourself wasting time on many easy but not important tasks. The second approach is called the MYE approach. Which is also an acronym for managing your execution. In fact, I believe that this represents the formula of successful productivity, describing it in the shortest way. It's about giving the right amount of energy and attention to the right tasks at the correct moment in time. This is important because it keeps your productivity performance high at all times. In the next chapter, we will look at the effects of categorizing your types of tasks and workload.

Categorizing The Types Of Tasks And Workload

I would like to start by answering why to categorize. We categorize so that we can understand, organize and manage large amounts of data. In this chapter, we'll look at ways to help you categorize your tasks and workload effectively. It's a normal and common way to simply categorize your tasks to the nature of its activity, for example, categorizing it as communication, creativity, financials etc.. Another example for this would be to categorize them into different areas of responsibilities, for example, your company, your NGO that you're involved in or your projects etc... The benefit of categorizing this way is that you can manage your attention and energy. However, this might get out of control if you have a lot of diverse areas of responsibilities.

Another way to categorize your tasks is by assessing the time it takes for completion. This is a great way to help you track and manage your time. It also gives you the opportunity to think about what tasks to execute and when. When prioritizing, the most important way to categorize your tasks and workload is by grouping your tasks to its result-oriented impacts. This is a great way to keep forward towards achieving your goals and objectives. Simply, you categorize your tasks into three different groups, zero effect tasks. Maintenance tasks and goal oriented tasks. Zero effect tasks are the things that you do that have no relation and impact whatsoever to your important goals and objectives.

For example, activities like watching TV or meeting up with your friends for a drink. These can be added to your to do lists and calendars as tasks and events, however, they mainly have no effect on achieving your important goals. This is why this group is called zero effect. The maintenance tasks are the things that you do to remain momentum when you are going forward towards your goals. Not all tasks we do at work directly affect the milestones of achieving goals. There are many things that we do so that we can keep doing the goal oriented tasks, for example, planning and scheduling the week, these are the tasks we do to keep maintaining the momentum for goal related tasks. This is why this group is called maintenance. Goals, related tasks add value to your milestones on your way to achieving goals. It is important that you don't procrastinate from doing these tasks.

In fact, these are the tasks that you should prioritize as much as possible. To be more precise, these are the tasks that have result oriented impacts, for example, sending out quotations for your services and products or working on marketing campaigns or closing a sale deal etc... These are the types of tasks that directly relate and add effect to your goals and objectives. Let's do a quick summary to conclude this chapter, you can simply categorize your tasks based on the nature of their activities or areas of responsibilities. This is a great way to see and manage your energy and attention. Similarly, you can categorize your tasks based on the time it takes for completion. This is a great way to help you track and manage your time. And finally, you can categorize your tasks based on their result-oriented impacts by grouping them to zero effects, maintenance and goal related tasks.

Performing a PDM Scan

To really assess and bring out your current priorities to life, it is essential that you have your tasks and events listed properly. Learning the method covered in this chapter will help you get ready for prioritizing effectively. It is crucial not to keep your responsibilities in your mind, but rather have them noted at a secure and easily accessible place. Sometimes, even though you would have your tasks noted and listed securely, you might find yourself out of focus and working on things that are not even on your list at all. This is a common indication that you do not have your tasks and workload listed accurately to keep you aligned with your priorities so that you don't skip any outstanding items you can perform at PDM scan on a regular basis depending on your productivity performance, once a day or once a week is great. PDM scan is made of a physical scan, a digital scan and a mind scan.

Physical scan is when you go through the physical items on your desk and work environment to identify any important notes or reminders to add to your list. For example, you saw an ad in the newspaper that caught your attention a few days ago, and you left it on your desk for a while and didn't yet do anything about it, or you noted that you would send an email to your colleague and it's still an outstanding task. Scan, identify and add all these to your PDM scan list. Digital scan is similar to a physical scan. This time you scan all your outstanding tasks by checking your digital environment, checking your Emails, Calendars, WhatsApp conversations or any digital platform you work on, simply; Scan, identify and add all these to your PDF scan list. One of the main reasons why you find yourself working on tasks that are not even listed on your to do list is because you keep them in your mind.

This is a very bad habit that directly affects your productivity in a negative way. Therefore, not skipping to perform a mind scan is very important. As mentioned before, your PDM scan list should be at a secure and easily accessible place so that you can easily add the items created or come to your mind. A great way for clearing your mind is by performing a method called Mind Sweep by David Allen, who states 'your mind is for having ideas, not holding them'. Let's do a quick summary to recap what we covered in this chapter. You must create a bank of responsibilities, tasks and events before you start prioritizing them. A method to successfully get prepared is by creating a PDM. scan list. A PDM scan consists of a physical scan, digital scan and a mind scan. You must do this on a regular basis, daily or weekly, depending on your productivity performance.

Make Prioritizing A Priority

Welcome to the third chapter of the Book. In this chapter, you will be introduced to three different prioritization methods and why you really need to make prioritizing a priority. First of all, making prioritizing a priority will enable you to naturally review your workload. The main aim is to get organized and plan your work effectively. Of course, there is a difference between a task that is urgent and a task that is important, an urgent task may not be very important. The most challenging part is to accurately prioritize more than one project's work. There are three methods covered in this chapter that will significantly help you make the correct decisions for different types of projects. We'll look at the Eisenhower metrics method. Ivy Lee method and M.I.T method.

3 Different Methods To Prioritize

Eisenhower metrics are all about the separation of urgent and important. It enables you to identify where your attention should really be. To be able to use this tool, you must apply all your tasks individually onto the metrics. You must identify how important and urgent each one is. Scaling from zero to 10. Once you have all your items on the metrics, you can see that your items are divided into four groups. Urgent and important. You must do this as soon as possible. Important, but not urgent. Decide when you'll do this and schedule them. Urgent, but not important, if you can delegate these tasks to someone else, then delegate them. If not, then try scheduling them to the earliest as possible, neither urgent nor important. Drop these tasks from your to do lists. Ivy Lee method. The Ivy Lee method is all about ranking the priority.

Typically, this is used for identifying the next day's tasks, you're right down the six most important things you want to accomplish tomorrow. It should not really be more than six and you should prioritize them in the order of their true importance. When you arrive tomorrow, focus only on these tasks and close the day by doing the same for the next day with unfinished items to be on the list and repeat this on every working day. M.I.T method. M.I.T method is also known as eating the frog method, this short statement by Mark Twain clearly explains the method. If you have to eat a live frog, it does not pay to sit and look at it for a very long time. Although this method is about mono-tasking. Technically, you focus on the most important task on your list until it's completed. For example, when a salesperson on duty starts helping a random customer that makes a visit to the store, the salesperson performs an M.I.T task by focusing on performing the necessary work until the sales process is completed.

Briefing Of Prioritization Process Workflow

Great job you are nearly halfway throughout the Book. In this chapter, you will learn the process of prioritizing, with an exclusively designed workflow ... the overall purpose of this workflow is to provide you with a conceptual framework that leads you step by step to prioritize the workload effectively. The process of the framework is made of systematically connected three stages. Therefore, it's important to apply the necessary processes when moving through the stages of the workflow. If you're ever unclear of what you should be doing at any time, use this framework as a reference tool to help you focus on what you need to do in each stage of the process.

Prioritization Process Workflow

In order to successfully prioritize, you must start with the first step of the process, which is to collect all your tasks you need to prioritize. By performing a PDM scan, you will not miss any outstanding tasks because you will scan your physical and digital environment as well as clearing your mind. At the completion of the first step, you will end up with a compiled random list of all your tasks. The next step of the process is to categorize. At this step, you transform your list to their result oriented impacts by grouping them to zero effect maintenance and goal related tasks. Of course, categorizing your tasks into three groups automatically clarifies what tasks you should prioritize and eliminate.

At the completion of step two, your list turns into three groups, eliminating the zero effect tasks, you take maintenance and goal related tasks to the next step of the process, which is to examine them. You examine by applying all your tasks individually onto Eisenhower metrics. The main outcome of this last step is to visualize your groups of tasks in four segments, which enables you to identify what tasks you do, schedule, delegate and eliminate. The tasks in urgent and important fit into the do segment, the tasks in important but not urgent fit into the schedule segment. The tasks in urgent but not important fit into the delegates segment and the tasks neither urgent nor important fit into the eliminate segment.

3 Rules Of Successful Time Management

You're doing very well now that we've completed all aspects of prioritization. We are ready to take a close look at what makes it possible for us to manage tasks and time effectively. Time management is the process of organizing and planning how to allocate your time between specific activities. Good time management enables you to work smarter, not harder, so that you get more done in less time. Failing to effectively manage time causes stress, especially when dealing with deadlines and pressures are high, time is the most precious asset. Everybody equally gets 24 hours in a day. However, it's a fact that knowing how to manage time effectively leads you to successful results. Certainly the most common benefits of time management are; to save time, reduce stress, get more done and to have more control on your functioning.

The most important question is how do you successfully manage time? The answer is by being able to give the right amount of energy and attention to the right task at the correct moment in time. And what makes this possible depends on how you plan and organize your time and actions. Of course, being busy does not mean being productive. So far in the previous chapters of this Book, you learned how to prioritize tasks by identifying what tasks to do, schedule, delegate and eliminate. The worst enemy when managing time is time waster and productivity-reducer tasks. And by prioritizing process workflow, you already eliminated these from your workloads.

Time management is simple, if you follow these three rules, you must plan and organize your actions and stick to your plan. Eliminate time waster and productivity-reducer tasks from your actions, give the right amount of energy and attention to the right task at the correct moment in time.

Planning With Etc And Energy Levels To Manage Time

To successfully manage time, don't let deadlines take control. You must have the control of your own actions. Managing your actions with ETC plays a big role. ETC is a value that is expressed in hours of work required to complete a task. It is an acronym for Estimated Time to Complete. Planning your actions with ETC allows you to organize your tasks and time. A simple yet very effective way to perform ETC is by categorizing your tasks into three different groups, tasks estimated to be completed in less than 20 minutes, tasks estimated to be completed between 20 minutes to an hour. And tasks estimated to be completed in more than an hour when planning your workload.

It's important to schedule your tasks effectively, knowing the approximate time it takes to complete. Each task enables you to decide what tasks to execute and when. The most effective way to schedule your tasks is by using your energy levels. Everybody has their own unique pattern of energy levels throughout the day. It's crucial to observe your energy levels and identify your highs and lows and a normal workday might look something like this. The method of effective scheduling is to allocate the right tasks to the correct moment in time, and this is possible by allocating Maintenance types of tasks to low energy time periods and Goal-Related types of tasks to high energy time periods.

What To Do Next? How To Keep Prioritized And Organized!

Congratulations, you are at the final stage of the Book. So far, we covered how to get prepared for prioritization, three types of prioritization methods, a step by step workflow process for prioritization and finally important aspects of time management. In this last chapter, we will take a close look at what makes it possible for us to keep ourselves well prioritized and well organized. It is important to be able to reflect on yourself occasionally, then give yourself a chance to change some of your actions, pushing them towards better behaviors and a well-designed feedback loop provides us just that. Therefore, pre-scheduling weekly review sessions for yourself makes a huge impact on keeping yourself well organized.

The main objectives of these scheduled weekly review sessions are to measure, adjust and develop your own weekly performance. A great recommendation is to implement the GTD Weekly Review designed by David Allen. It consists of the following steps. Step one, collect all your loose papers and put them into your basket for processing. Step two, process your notes to clean any action items, appointments, new projects etc.. Step three, review your previous calendars to remind yourself of any ideas or tasks that you might have skipped. Step four, review your upcoming calendar to see if there are any new actions you need to add to your lists. Step five. Into your head, write down anything that is currently in your mind or capturing your attention.

Step six, review your projects list to determine each project's status and if there are any actions you might need to take. Step seven, review your next action lists, bring them up to date by marking them off as completed, use completed actions as triggers to remind you of any further steps you might need to take. Step eight, review your waiting for lists and check off anything that has been already received. Step nine. Review any relevant checklists. Step 10, review your someday list and decide if there is anything you're ready to move onto your active projects list. Step 11, review your project's support files to make sure you haven't missed any new actions you needed to take. And finally, step 12, be creative. Take your time to brainstorm new ideas. Give yourself the chance to get creative and reflect on your dreams.

Key Takeaway: Formula Of Successful Productivity

Let's conclude the Book with the most important takeaway: everything you learned in this Book helps you to get organized and manage your time effectively and always remember that the main aim is to be able to give the right amount of energy and attention to the correct tasks at the correct moment in time. ... And that's the formula of successful productivity.

What Next

Congratulations, you made it. Thank you for reading this Book. Now go and implement what you've learned so far. Please feel free to send me any questions you might have. I'll be happy to answer them.

Why Are Certifications The Best Way To Learn It Skills?

In this chapter, will you certifications as core vehicles for learning, we won't focus just on minimizing time to certification, though we will use certification as a basis for building super learning systems, for keeping your skills relevant. There are many benefits to getting certified. The first benefit of getting certified is that it gives you a clear goal for your learning efforts. The Internet is full of possibilities and material for honing your technical skills. It can be challenging to choose a topic and an appropriate scale and depth for your learning efforts. Setting a goal for getting certified gives you a topic, a scope and a depth you can cover in a reasonable time. You can think of it as your definition of having a clear goal that's not too far off, but pushes you enough to focus for the weeks or months required to get there.

The second benefit is that a preparation for a certification will give you comprehensive coverage on the chosen subject. If you start learning by focusing on your task at hand, for example, a project in your current role or based only on your niche interest at any given time, you can miss basic understanding of some important, maybe not the most interesting basic aspects of the chosen subject. Avoiding these kinds of blind spots and knowing what there is to know, knowing what you don't know is usually seen as a benefit of having a formal education in your profession. The same can be at least partly achieved by getting certified. Third, there are a lot of good quality resources available for certification preparation on the Internet.

Go on Amazon.com and you'll find plenty of choices for reading and a variety of practice tests for your chosen certification. You'll find that they cover almost any certification topic you can imagine at a fraction of the cost compared to traditional classroom learning. Fourth is feedback. Feedback is important for your motivation. If you just browse, read and play on the topic on your own, the progress may feel slow and unvalidated. Without feedback, you'll miss the sense of progress and you may lose motivation. Certification will give you feedback and this sense of accomplishment will boost your confidence and keep you going.

Finally, getting a certificate is a way of marketing your skills. It can be argued whether having a certificate really tells how skillful you are. A certificate can be just a first step and just enough skills to overcome the friction of getting up to speed with a new topic. But from the customer's point of view, whether it's the employer or the client for your consulting engagement, hiring a certified IT professional is a lower risk than hiring a non certified professional. And guess what? You'll see that reflected in your compensation as well.

What Are The Top Paying It Certifications?

Speaking of compensation, certifications have real value in global knowledge 2020, IT skills and salary survey Google certified professional cloud architect was the highest paying certification for the second year in a row, paying an average salary of one hundred seventy five thousand seven hundred sixty one dollars.

However, getting certified in a single topic is not the perfect plan for your career, and to systematize the learning and certification efforts, you should carefully choose the topics so that they form a hole that is more valuable than individual certifications alone.

In this chapter, I decided to call chosen topics a career focus.

How To Choose A Motivating And Future Proof Certification Path?

In a world of it, opportunities are endless, this might make choosing a career focused, challenging. One thing is for sure, you can't handle and keep up to date with everything you need to choose. Let's introduce my method for choosing a career focus first list the IT skills you feel naturally drawn to. Don't think too much about it. Just list 10 to 20 topics. What you would like to learn if you had freedom to choose whatever. For example, python programming, Google Cloud platform, health care. I noticed that the topics you feel interested in are usually ones you're good at or that you'll feel motivated to learn. Next, take a step back and investigate the list.

Try to look for overlapping areas that would form a bigger hole. We're not looking for a life changing life calling, but a practical theme of interest for the next steps of your career. It should be a bit higher level than a specific skill, like programming with a specific language, something you could master in three to five years. This is what I call a career focus. In my experience, this is about a good time frame to plan your career in. It's hard to predict the longer term, but three to five years is quite predictable. Now you have a list of interests and rough ideas for your career. Focus for at least the next few years. Let's tie it to market demand. Think about what is hot in your professional environment in the next three to five years.

What is the world demanding? What are the industries that will be ramping up investments in it in coming years? What are the technologies that are already being used and likely to expand exponentially in the coming years? What kinds of skills are in short supply? What kind of companies are hiring and more specifically, which ones are having trouble hiring? Next, compare this with your interests and themes you are thinking about for your career focus. Try to find one interesting career focus area and give it a name. For example, a title in our example. It could be a healthcare cloud architect. Now you have a career focus for the next three to five years. Let this be the focus which you'll mirror your super learning skills and the system we cover in this chapter.

Where To Start For The Biggest Return On Investment?

The next question is whether what topic you should start with and whether you should acquire wide general skills or dive deep on a single topic, there are different types of skills, wide and deep. Having deep expertise on a single topic can be a lucrative thing. But as technology is developing fast, it can also lead to a dead end. You can avoid the dead end by focusing on a wider but more shallow set of skills. It gives you more options. However, general level technical skills are not as valuable as deep skills in some niche areas. It's also hard to store your skills for later use. It's more or less use it or lose it. You tend to forget what you don't use. One way to think about this challenge is the TI model. In the TI model, you acquire deep skills on one or over time a couple of skills and wider but more shallow understanding on a wide set of topics.

This gives you both deep, valuable skills and more options to go into new areas if you run into dead ends in your chosen area of deep focus. Now reflecting this to certifications, getting certified in a variety of topics is a good way to get your high level understanding wide and up to date. This would be a kind of insurance which will open new career options if you get stuck in your current role. But widening your options should not overrun the utmost importance of performing well at your current role. In this deep side, getting certified is a good way to get over the friction of getting started up to speed and gaining a wider perspective on the topics that are important at your current role.

After getting up to speed with the immediate requirements for your current role, it should motivate you to keep up the momentum, dig deeper and gain deep skills on what you're currently working on while also giving hands on practice that makes the skill more permanent. My recommendation is that you should choose the first topics to study, depending on how comfortable you feel with your skills in your current role. If you feel that getting a bit of confidence in your current role would not harm, we suggest starting with the deep skills on the vertical bar of the team model based on the requirements at hand in your current role.

But if your daily work is an effortless routine for you at the moment, maybe it could be a good time to widen your perspective and focus on the skills at the horizontal bar of the team model. For our example, let's focus on health care cloud architecture. Our hero could be working as an application development consultant for a health care customer who is looking into cloud options and possibly using Google Cloud platform for other applications, which on the other hand could be new to our hero. Then it could make sense for our hero to choose to start with something that is close to what he needs at the moment, which would make learning immediately useful and gives us energy to proceed.

For example, our hero could choose to get certified with Google Cloud, with Google Cloud Certified Cloud Engineer certification, which is a general level certification, giving him a good overview of Google cloud platforms. Now it's time for you to choose a certificate matching your chosen career focus. Don't hurry with this. Take your time to consider and investigate different options and possibly build a certification roadmap by putting the interesting option on timeline.

What Defines How We Behave And The Results?

The short term goal, your daily grind, this is the thing that drives you towards your main goal, it's what you should focus on and not to continually worry too much about your medium or long term goals. Let's elaborate a bit on this. Whatever you do, sales, studying or exercising, you don't really have power to decide the outcomes. What you can control is your actions. The process of taking small steps in the right direction will improve the probability of a good outcome. But ultimately, the outcome is outside of your direct control. Still, we tend to give the outcome too much energy and focus. Dreaming about the long term results can cause us to lose the focus on taking the right small steps every day.

Focusing too much on outcome and progress can result in, for example, that we need to succeed over our expectations. In the short term, we get too excited and lose focus on our daily progress. Or if we don't progress as planned, we lose our trust and we stop. The secret is that it's better to focus on the process. Daily progress one step at a time. Big goals are achieved one step at a time. If you take care of small things, big things take care of themselves generally. Now what we do is particularly determined by our identity. If we face a new situation, we first think about our identity. What kind of person am I? What would a person like me do in this kind of situation? Our actions are driven by our identity. It also works, vice versa.

Our identity is formed a lot based on how we act. This is a self enforcing loop. If you form an effective learning habit, it will change your identity. You'll think of yourself as and become a super learner and it will again make the learning habits stick. Some like to say fake it till you make it. The key is to get started and to keep showing up. Don't set too high a goal in the beginning. Showing up daily and achieving your moderate goals keeps you going and builds momentum. Success drives self-confidence and keeps the wheels spinning. Success builds success. If you're not yet sold on the power of identity, think of a scenario where you would be deprived of sleep for months. You would be shouted at and you might not be given any privacy or time alone, even when going to the bathroom.

Would this be a motivating state for you? How about if we attach a meaningful identity to these struggles? How about if these horrible struggles were due to being a mother? How does the identity of being a mother change the situation? Identity is at the core of what we do daily and what we do daily drives the outcomes we get. What this means from our career perspective is that as we're living in a volatile, uncertain, complex and ambiguous world and the average half life of a skill in it is shortening in an ever increasing speed, we should see learning as a key part of our professional identity. We'll never be ready as IT professionals.

We should not value our professional capital based just on what we know or can do. But a big part of being an IT professional is being good at learning. Learning. You should be a big part of our identity and daily life as IT professionals. And this is the idea, continuous learning as part of your daily life.

And it is at the core of the system that will build for you in this Book before continuing one point about identity. Identity has a social aspect. We follow other people, especially in new, uncertain situations. We look for examples from others. As marketing guru Seth Godin puts it, identity is people liking us to things like this.

We are hardwired to follow the habits of our tribe. In Hunter-Gatherer times, being abandoned from our tribe was a death sentence. We are evolutionarily programmed to follow the standards of our tribe and deviation from those standards will make us feel bad and ashamed. To be more specific, breaking apart could be challenging. Identifying with new tribes helps. Being open and just acting based on our aspirational identity also helps.

It Is All About The Mindset!

One core aspect of identity is our mindset, our mindset is our collection of thoughts and beliefs that shape our identity. The mindset affects how we think, what we feel and what we do. According to researcher Carol Dweck, there are two types of mindsets: a fixed mindset and a growth mindset. People with a growth mindset have an underlying belief that their learning and intelligence can grow with time and experience. In contrast, people with a fixed mindset believe that their basic abilities, intelligence and talents are fixed traits. They think that we're born with a certain amount, and that's all we have with a growth mindset.

People believe their abilities and intelligence can be developed with effort, learning and persistence. Their basic abilities are simply a starting point for their potential. They don't believe everyone is the same, but they hold on to the idea that everyone can learn and become better if they try. Fixed beliefs will hold us back from making change. If we have a trait that we believe cannot be changed, such as our intelligence, our weight or our bad habits, we will avoid situations that could possibly be uncomfortable or that we think are useless. Douek found out that having a growth mindset is the key starting point.

If we want to succeed in any aspect of our life, early or effortless success can kill our long term achievement by highlighting a fixed mindset. But if our success is achieved with struggle, we learn to value and believe in effort and build a growth mindset. As it said. Whether you believe you can do a thing or not, you are right. With this attitude, you never fail. You either win or learn. Let's rehearse. We should have learning at the core of our identity and focus on daily grind, not the long term goals or outcomes, but how do we keep up the motivation?

External Motivation And Hidden Cost Of Doing Nothing

How do we muster up the motivation to focus on the daily grind long enough to reach our goals? It's a good idea to sit down for a moment and clarify our motivations before we start the grind. It might even be worth writing them down so that we can rehearse them when we need a bit of push to keep going. Generally, motivation can be divided into two categories, external and internal. We have already touched the external motivators for certifications such as a lucrative earning potential, social respect and career safety. External motivation can be further divided into two categories in things we aim towards and in things we want to stay away from.

Which is your motivation? Are you looking to get rid of something or striving to gain something? The secret is that by nature we are very fearful. We are more fearful of losing something than we are inclined to take risks to gain something. This tendency makes making choices hard. If we choose something, we lose all the other options. This also leads to certain friction against approaching something new. Not making a choice at all is easier. This is why one important aspect to consider about external motivators is the cost of doing nothing or the cost of delay. Choosing not to do anything is also a choice, and it usually means losing an opportunity, especially as the value of our skills decreases at increasing speeds.

The cost of doing nothing, not keeping up with continuous learning is likely to mean that we hit a dead end in our I.T. career sooner than we imagine. External motivation is limited when we have the basics like physical and social safety in place. We don't get more motivation with more external motivators. For example, based on research in the U.S., this would be about seventy five thousand dollars in a year, after which earning more doesn't add more motivation. And we need to look into other factors. This is when we need to look for internal motivators to keep the motivation up. Internal motivation consists of three main drivers: autonomy, mastery and purpose.

Circles Of Influence: How To Learn Optimism?

Autonomy, the feeling of being in control of your own life is a key driver for motivation. This becomes clear if you think the opposite. If you're not in control, what happens? Why even bother when you feel that we're in control and can influence what happens? Outcomes depend on our choices. We naturally take responsibility for our actions. Control can be thought of in three layers. First, there are things in which we don't have any power to decide or influence the current economic climate, for instance. Second, there are things which we can influence but don't decide, for example, your health, your success or your employer.

Third, there are things in which we can influence and we can decide, for example, putting in 30 minute efforts to study for certification every day. If we focus our efforts on or worry about things we can't decide or influence, we'll lose our motivation and become cynical or depressed. We'll learn that your actions don't matter. This is what Martin Seligman calls learned helplessness. But if we focus on things, we decide things that are directly under our control. There's correlation between our actions and outcome. We start to build momentum, self-confidence and motivation.

Linear, Logarithmic And Exponential Growth

Second to the internal motivators is mastery, this is about a sense of progress, if the task at hand is too easy, we get bored. It doesn't feel like we're making progress. If it's too hard, we don't get those small doses of dopamine from succeeding in something. According to fellow researchers, tasks should be about four percent above our current level of performance so that we need to get outside our comfort zone and get our capabilities and use, but not too much. We tend to think progress is linear, but that's rarely the case. There are different kinds of growth. First, there are things that grow logarithmically in a logarithmic growth. We see a lot of progress in the beginning, but continuing progress is difficult. As an example, we could think about athletic performance or weight loss.

In these, there are natural limits for growth that will slow the progress at some point since logarithmic growth is steep in the beginning. It also implies that it's easier to slide back down the hill. Carelessness can mean the immediate gains that are easy to get in the beginning are often easily lost as well. What we would like to have, however, is exponential growth and compound interest. As an example, we could think about investing or building a personal brand here. The key is to build momentum by starting with a low enough goal and not raising the goal too much at a time. This way will get constant success, which will build our self-confidence and identity over time and keep the momentum going.

The compound interest of targeting only four percent above our current level of performance, as the flow researchers suggest, will create a compound interest which over time will surprise us with compound interest. Our progress will start slowly but accelerate at exponential speed. For example, one percent decrease every day would mean going down from one hundred percent to three percent in a year, while one percent increase every day would end in three thousand seven hundred eighty percent in a year. Daily grind matters here. Exponential curves are somewhat rarer than logarithmic ones. For example, in your learning effort, it's likely that it will lead to a logarithmic curve at some point and growth of your skill level will slow down significantly at some point.

After that, you need perseverance to keep going. And if you stop, you're at risk of sliding back down. The hill will cover how to stay on an exponential path later in this chapter. But one key thing to remember here is that expecting linear growth when it's actually exponential causes many people to give up before they reach the accelerating returns. So whether growth is logarithmic or exponential, it's all about focus and patience. Stay on the track and it will pay off.

What Makes The Effort Meaningful?

At the very highest level of internal motivation is purpose, our professional lives take a huge part of our lives and in the long run, we need to feel our effort is meaningful to keep up the motivation. What gives our chosen career purpose? Purpose comes from outside us, from how our effort affects other people, our family, tribe or society in general. What are the big issues? Our daily grind is alleviating. We easily think about our professional role and its immediate context, how our role affects our close colleagues. But it's good to think further away every now and then. What meaning does our role have for our company? What meaning our company has in society and so on.

In our chosen example, our hero health care cloud specialist could remind himself that building better healthcare, it helps free health care professionals time from administrative tasks to taking care of patients, soothing the growing shortage of healthcare professionals due to aging populations such as his own parents. It's a good idea to connect the dots every now and then to pause and remind ourselves why even the small role we're playing is meaningful in the big picture. OK, that was a lot about motivation, but it's important. Spend a little time thinking about these motivational factors and write them down, preferably on paper, and return to them when you have a hard time keeping up with the daily grind or when you've lost the path and need to get back on track. Or why not rehearse the motivation as part of your daily learning ritual?

How To Automate The Learning?

As you remember, the key for success was that we should focus on the process, the daily grind and not the outcome, learning, sharpening the saw should become part of our identity and daily effort as IT professionals, as the learning is part of our professional identity, our daily work, we are never ready then. It's not really a question of pushing ourselves hard to nail the next certification in a record time, but more a question of how much we should invest every day in our learning. How big should the part of our daily life be consumed by learning? Is it 30 minutes, an hour or more? And how do we build a habit out of the daily grind? Habits are automatic actions we do without spending much energy.

As Daniel Kahneman said in his famous book, Thinking Fast and Slow, our brains have two operating systems system one and system two. System two is conscious, rational thinking. It's slow and effortful. It is the part of the brain that is self-aware, logical and skeptical. It makes up only two percent of our thinking. We are well aware of System two, however. System one is where almost 98 percent of our thinking happens and it is unconscious, automatic and effortless habits are part of system one. Habits are also the way in which we, with our limited, effortful but conscious system two can program system one and exploit its fast and effortless ability to assess what you should do in any given situation.

From evolution's point of view, habits are the brain's way to save energy in the world with limited resources. In short, habits are our brain's shortcuts. They enable us to think and analyze our actions in every situation with habits, we can act quick and effortlessly. Habits operate by associating a cue to a desired outcome. The brain's mechanism to pick up cues that predict desirable outcomes and reinforce related actions is called a habit loop. The habit loop contains four parts: cue craving, response and reward. First, there is a cue. Our brain is constantly scanning the environment and predicting what might happen next. Cues can be external or internal.

External cues come in through our senses, something we see, hear, smell, taste or even kinetic scents from body movement or positions. Cues can also be internal. For example, we can start to feel anxiety if we can't quite grasp the topic we are trying to learn. This uncomfortable feeling might trigger us to lose focus and make us look for something to comfort us. For example, to find something to eat. We usually think about cues as something clear and external, a phone vibrating in your pocket as a sign of a new message. For instance, however, the most common cues are related to time and location.

We tend to do the same things in certain times and in certain locations. This is why implementation intentions are so powerful. Implementation intention is a plan you make beforehand about when and where to act a certain way. Too often we try to change our habits without being specific enough about what, when and where we will change. We promised that we're going to lose weight, study this and that topic, or get certified in something. But we rarely state when and where that is going to take place and then it never takes place. This applies especially to things that take time, things that can't be done in one sitting when the inspiration hits, things that are important but not urgent.

Exercise and studying are examples of things that require consistent repetition of small batches of effort. Studies show that implementation intention is the most important principle for building this kind of habit. For example, for learning or exercising implementation intention states. I will do X behavior at X time in X location. James Clear guides us in his excellent book, Atomic Habits. The key principles with cues is to make use obvious and vice versa, to get rid of bad habits, hide cues that lead to undesired outcomes. For example, don't buy any snack foods for home. If you want to stop snacking or place your running gear on the front of your door, if you want to improve the probability that you will go jogging.

The second component of the habit loop is the desire. In our opinion, this is the least understood part of the habit loop. Habit doesn't just jump directly from cue to action and reward as the habit loop is commonly understood. Neurochemically the reward is a small dose of dopamine, the same chemical which is behind cocaine. Dopamine is a good hormone, but it also improves focus, learning and pattern recognition. It's the brain's way to evaluate and program what is worth doing. As we do something worth repeating, we get the reward in the form of a small dose of dopamine, which helps to store this cue reward relationship in our memory. But next time, and after multiple repetitions, we will get a hit of dopamine directly from the cue.

There is no need for reward. This is where the desire or craving gets in the picture. In the desire phase, dopamine is pushing us to act in response to a cue. Now, the big thing is that the dopamine boost that we get in the desire phase of the habit loop is bigger than the dopamine shot we get with the reward. This is what makes our habits stick and drives us to act based on the cue. This also means that over time, even if we don't get reward from the action anymore, we're still getting the dopamine shot from the cue, for example, we could get so used to alcohol that it doesn't give us any reward anymore. It doesn't make us feel good. But the cue, for example, the feeling of opening a beer can is still driving the habit through the mechanism of dopamine.

This could mean that we get addicted to the cue opening the beer can and not in the reward itself. The alcohol, according to James Clear. The key to optimizing desire or cravings is to make the desirable habit attractive. For example, associate daily learning with the first cup of coffee for the day and the opposite for habits you want to get rid of. For example, commit to smell sour herring after slipping into a bad habit of snacking to associate it with something undesirable. Third part of the habit loop is the action we feel compelled to do with the cue as we remember the environment, and the time is quite often the cue driving our action, not our willpower.

As an example, if we want to start our day by spending 30 minutes studying, we could build sitting down at our desk in the morning as the cue to start the habit of studying. If we constantly study as the first thing in the day as the environment is driving our actions, this also means that the organization culture can concretely stick in the walls of the office. Sometimes it's a good idea to change the environment, to change the habits both at individual levels or at an organizational level. James Clear guides us to make the action or response to a cue as easy as possible to implement to increase the likelihood of it taking place. This can be naturally understood from the biological perspective.

We are energy saving organisms that tend to follow the path of least resistance. If you want to study every morning, make everything ready the night before, have a clear plan goal and a to -do list about what you will work on the next morning to avoid uncomfortable ambiguity, which raises the threshold to start or the opposite. If you want to get rid of checking social media on your phone too often while studying, place your phone out of reach to make the bad habit harder. Then we get the reward that is important, especially in early stages of habit building here. The challenge is that we tend to value immediate rewards over delayed rewards. We can help this by finding immediate rewards on the way to delayed rewards. For example, we can have the first cup of coffee after the daily morning studying session as an immediate reward.

Just getting anything done and checking that item on our To-Do list will work as a reward and give a shot of dopamine as well. As we remember, dopamine drives focus and action. So from this point as well, it is important to start our day with something that gives you the first shots of dopamine so that you can start your daily upward spiral of productivity. Last, I would like to remind you that probably the most important aspect of habit creation is that you decide when and where you will do your learning. I would recommend doing it as the first thing every morning before the start of daily duties and before your mind gets cluttered with all the daily tasks and interruptions.

How To Keep On The Exponential Learning Path?

What is the best way to program our fast and energy efficient system one or form our habits? You've probably heard about the 10,000 hours of practice Kay Anders Ericsson studied that Malcolm Gladwell made famous in his best selling book, Outliers. Ericsson studied top performers in different fields and came to the conclusion that to get to the top of any given field requires 10000 hours of practice. The 10,000 hours has been debated a lot. However, the amount of hours is not as interesting as the way of practice Erikson found out to be the most effective. It's called deliberate practice. You might remember that when we spoke about exponential growth and logarithmic growth, I promised to tell you a way to keep on an exponential growth path in learning as long as possible.

Deliberate practice is the way to avoid falling in diminishing returns of logarithmic growth and keep growing. The key point of deliberate practice is that mindless, habitual repetition does not bring results. As it said, repetition is the mother of retention. But it also means repetition does not make perfect. It is permanent. The practice should be conducted very mindfully so that it will improve our abilities, not just make our bad habits stick. Beware what you repeat. Each practice session should be mindfully focused and have a specific goal of improving some specific aspects of performance. We should have a plan with a target for each practice session to produce a specific response or learning effect.

For example, while practicing tennis, learning backhand drive could be first repeated very slowly for many times, making sure it goes right and so that we are programmed to perform it correctly, then slowly adding speed and force, making sure that we don't make the wrong way of doing it stick. Too often we assume that we're getting better simply because we're gaining more experience. In reality, we could be merely reinforcing our current habits, not improving them. Let's go through the process of deliberate practice first. We need best practices. Usually there are best practices in our field or industry or even in our life that have been shown to work as humans. We are risk aware and have a tendency to ponder about what might not work paralysis by analysis.

But we should really rather scale what works. So learn the basics of your draft and build a mental model of exceptional performance. Try to be specific. The less ambiguous it is, the harder it is for your mind to get stuck in paralysis. Second, stop before each repetition and think about what you're trying to do and how often this is done with a coach. The goal should be to challenge the status quo, be just outside your comfort zone. Not too hard, but not too easy for you to slip in automatic habits, for example, four percent harder than your current skill level as it is said to be the prescription for follow. Third, focused activity. Deliberate practice requires your full attention with maximal, mental and or physical effort for feedback. Without feedback, you cannot figure out what you need to improve on or how close you are to achieving your goals.

Feedback gives you a realistic view of your progress, whether a coach, a mentor or peer or some form of self assessment, you need a means of pinpointing your strengths and weaknesses. This is the only way to identify and work through trouble spots and keep on the growth curve. You cannot start from where you are. Not yet be humble and patient. Adding four percent constantly will take you forward faster than you are afraid of, but you need to start from a realistic level. Fifth, recovery. The focus and effort required in deliberate practice can only be sustained for a short period of time. The level of intensity and concentration makes recovery time important.

Laboratory studies of extended practice have capped the optimal time at one hour per day, three to five days a week, and real life studies have seen reduced benefits when practice sessions exceed two hours. Last repetition the key aspects of deliberate practice. What makes it so effective is its regularity. Erickson and his colleagues found out that top performers, no matter their area of expertise, kept a similar practice regimen brief but intense, often daily or semi-weekly sessions. Deliberate practice is a long term investment in improving yourself and your capabilities.

How to feel and perform at your best?

If deliberate practice is the key in programming our habits and unconscious system one, what is the best way to get and perform what we have learned? While programming system one is conscious and effortful, being managed by a slow and effortful system is on the way when we want to perform at our best. When we perform, we need to get our thinking mind system out of the way. We need to get into flow. Flow is the optimal state of performance where you feel your best and perform your best in flow. We get so focused on the task at hand that everything else disappears. We get our full capacity, our full programming in use, our action and awareness merge, our sense of self vanishes, our sense of time distorts, and all aspects of our performance go through the roof. Some call flow, the peak experience or being in the zone.

It is not just an optimal state for performance, it's also an optimal state of being. It feels good if you've experienced runner's high. It's a form of flow flow, a term which was originally formed by McColley Six sent me Whouley in his research of happiness to describe a state that was consistently described by his research subject as experience, where every decision, every action flows seamlessly, perfectly and effortlessly. How do you get into flow? Follow the flow cycle. Struggle is the first phase of the flow cycle. In this phase, we absorb the information we need to be able to piece together what it means to try and tackle the challenge in front of us during this phase in order to amp up focus and alertness.

Stress hormones like cortisol, adrenaline and no repeat offering are pumped into the system. Tension rises, frustration as well. The key to get into flow is to not give in to the frustration. When you're trying to get into flow and frustration hits, it's all too easy to find distraction. For instance, go to check your social media. In a study, developers found that getting back into flow after distraction takes on average. Twenty five minutes. So thirty seconds on Twitter is not just thirty seconds down the drain. It's a full twenty five minutes and thirty seconds. And the worst part is that you're not able to persist in the struggle. It might mean you never get into optimal state of being and performance and the flow. Second stage, if you feel like you're hitting a wall, that's a good thing. Stop what you're doing.

Take a breath or walk away for a minute and just think of something else. Do something fun that doesn't challenge you too much. In order to get ourselves into flow, we need a pattern to disrupt. We need to relax and release the tension we build in the first phase. With the release, we trigger an important chemical shift in the brain. Nitric oxide floods the system. This relieves us from the stress hormones, cortisol and no epinephrine that previously flooded the system during the struggle phase. Now we have the space required for dopamine and endorphins to make their way into the scene and we get into flow. Third stage is flow. Now, you go back to the task you were previously working on and you will get absorbed in the complete focus and flow.

Struggle gives way to release, which creates the space for flow. You're in the zone in a state where you feel and perform at your best. Your brain is flooded with a cocktail of neurotransmitters and you're in an elusive state. We all seek to find fourth stage recovery as a deliberate practice. The flow takes a big toll in our central nervous system and body. It requires a ton of resources and taps into reserves. We've been building up for a long time in preparation for flow. Needless to say, it takes a while for the body to recover and replenish. Give your body the time that it deserves and don't rush back into the next struggle phase so quickly.

Remember to take care of your physical needs: sleep, nutrition and fluid balance, exercise or movement and stress balance. OK, that was the flow cycle. Now researchers have also found triggers that can be used as a hack to help getting into flow. Essentially, flow can only arise when all of our attention is focused in the present moment. So that's what these triggers do. They drive attention into the here and now. The most important triggers are complete focus on the present moment, immediate feedback and immediate consequences. For example, taking the certification test, clear goals. For example, what we will be focused on for the next 30 minutes, the challenge skills ratio, four percent outside our comfort zone.

As mentioned before, high consequences risk physical, mental or social, deep embodiment. For example, learning by doing a rich environment, novelty, complexity that needs our full attention, creativity, especially pattern recognition or connecting new ideas. Flow is a huge topic. For example, there are separate ones for group flow and so on. I would suggest learning more about flow. I have attached some links to interesting resources in the chapter resources.

Top 3 Not Well Known Basics Of Learning

Now, finally, we get into the theory of learning. There are some fundamental misunderstandings people have about how we learn that leads people to measure their effort and progress in learning with vanilla metrics. People spend time on activities that feel productive but don't actually bring results. To avoid this trap will cover the science of learning.

You need to understand to unleash it. Learning capacity to its full potential first will cover how the memory really develops and fix the biggest misunderstanding people have about learning. Second, will cover the secret of permanent learning and fix the second learning trap.

People tend to fall in and lose a lot of effort used in learning. Third, we'll cover how the mind, with its limited capability, manages the complexity, which is especially important in learning information technology related topics. Let's get started.

The Biggest Misunderstanding About Learning

We have two types of memory, working memory, which deals with things on stage of the conscious mind, for example, words we're reading at any given moment. And then we have the second kind of memory, long term memory, which is for remembering things in the long run. Remembering something means that you can recall it from the long term memory. Our biggest mistake in learning is that we think that long term memory develops by putting something in memory. Yes, we can get something in our working memory by reading or reading, but this doesn't mean that it would be stored in the long term memory. In all learning, there is a specificity effect. You develop or learn what you practice.

This means that long term memory develops by getting something out of memory, not putting something in. We develop long term memory with active recall. This also means that forgetting is a prerequisite of learning. Before you can practice recalling something from long term memory to our working memory, we need to empty our working memory. Otherwise we're just turning around things. In your working memory. Learning requires effort. It is hard work. Just reading something and nodding along doesn't mean that you actually will remember it without effort. You do not develop the neural pathways that make it stick. The best way to remember is to do active recall and the best way to do active recall is to explain a concept out loud without relying on notes or material.

Explaining something in your own words requires effort which makes it stick. You can, for example, ask a friend to listen and evaluate if your explanation makes sense or record yourself with a mobile phone active recall by just thinking about how you would explain something that is too vague and doesn't provide the same results. Another option for explaining out loud is to write down the explanation, but it's not as effective as explaining out loud active recall. There's effort and many skip it, for example, by just rereading the material, which is easier but a total waste of time. Think of it as going to the mind. Gym effort matters.

Repetition matters. We can also think of long term memory as that fast and effortless system one and working memory as conscious and slow system too. And as we remember programming the systems, one is done by building habits. Let's look a bit deeper into System two or the long term memory. And in this context, how the recall from long term memory works is like fishing with an anchor that has many hooks. Memory works by association. If we activate a node in our memory, it will activate associated nodes. More association. We have to try to remember the more hooks or anchors it has. It is like a habit. Associations are like a cue that activates the neural pathways around it. These associations are related to our senses.

So having taste, smell, movement, rhythm, meaning the more senses there are associated with the thing we're trying to remember, the easier it is to fish that from the long term memory. Second key to making things stick in addition to association are stories where we only remember meaningful things. Our unconsciousness gives meaning to things through stories. Stories are a logical part of human evolution, as the basic structure of a story is something that has helped us survive. As we learn with habits, our mind is constantly scanning the environment and forecasting what happens next and how we should act to avoid threats or get rewards. Environmental cues can trigger different kinds of learning patterns on how to act.

These patterns are stored in our brain in the form of a story. Storing needs at least three components. First, in a good story, there's a subject that we associate ourselves with. We feel like the story would happen to us. Second, there's a threat towards that subject which creates tension and grabs our attention. Third, the tension intensifies and then it's released. This structure is efficiently stored in our memory as it gives us a powerful emotional lesson about how to manage some external threat and get away from it. Stories have helped our species to accelerate evolution. Stories spread faster than genes. Stories are part of cultural evolution. The body doesn't differentiate real experience and imagination.

One. The power of stories is that with a story we can learn, build habits or program the system, one from the experience of others, even previous generations. The power of stories for learning can be seen in neurochemistry as well. First, oxytocin enables us to identify with the protagonist to feel empathy. And when we face a threat in the story, we get into a state of stress that is flight or fight. Our body secretes stress hormones, cortisol which is catabolic and tears down our old ways of thinking. Also, on a neuro structural level with cortisol, we stay attentive to the threats in our environment and in the story following the resolution. Dopamine makes us feel good and reinforces our learning and focus on the new brain pathways.

The Secret Of Permanent Learning

Nugget of science and learning is repetition is the mother of learning, but as we remember from deliberate practice, practice doesn't make perfect, it makes permanent. When we learn something, we start forgetting it immediately. If we review, the thing we learned will not just reset our learning to the same state as it was after the first round of learning, but will also lower the rate of forgetting. The forgetting curve will start to flatten and we'll remember more in the long run. Now we get into the second learning trap. Many of us have learned a bad habit of trying to get through a test with a deadline miracle by filling the brain by studying over a short period of time last week, last day or even last night, a.k.a.

cramming this way. We can get through the test, but it doesn't create a long term memory of the topic. With the same effort over a longer period of time, learning would be less stressful and also make the topic stick in the long run in which you get the real value of even trying to learn. Just getting a certificate with the deadline, Myracle can feel nice and bring some status. But if you forget what you learn quickly, it just increases the imposter syndrome and creates stress as you're expected to deliver on the promise of being certified. Why not use the same amount of learning time more efficiently by spreading across a longer period, which would also create the long term memory of the topic? This curve of forgetting can be optimized with a spaced repetition schedule.

Important thing to notice is that this repetition should be done with active recall. When you review, beware of illusion, of competence. If we review something by just rereading or reading it, we're just reactivating it from the material to our working memory. While doing this a second or third time, it starts to feel familiar as we've read it before. This can give us a false illusion of competence. The material might feel familiar, but we would not actually be able to recall the topic from long term memory. We're just re-entering it into our working memory from external cues.

What is the optimal interval for spaced repetition? The best guidance I can give is that, as you might remember, it is important that we forget the topic before we can do our active recall practice with forgetting, I mean that it should not be actively present in our working memory so that we need effort to fetch it back from the long term memory. Mind has two modes of thinking, focused focus, thinking and diffused thinking. Again, you could think of them as the system one and two focus states are, as I said, focused, conscious and logical. While diffused mode. Our mind wanders freely, diffused mode gets activated while we do something that doesn't need our conscious attention.

For example, while walking or sleeping. The key is that our mind digests and integrates what we learned in the diffused mode. Hence, we should think of our learning a bit like exercise muscles don't grow while you exercise. Exercise breaks muscle and we need recovery. And it's during recovery. When we overcompensate for the damage done by exercise, we should think the same way. When we want to learn something, we need spurts of learning in focus states and then recovery in diffused states. Diffuse state also helps in emptying our working memory for the next round of practice. As you remember, forgetting is a prerequisite for learning. Avoid just pushing in new information.

As Erikson found, with deliberate practice, there is maximum. What mind can take in could be one to two hours a day. Spaced repetition is like working in a gym. According to super compensation theory, muscles grow when we recover, not when we're working out. The same is true with your mind. We stress the mind with new studying new information and we need to recover and let our unconscious mind process the information before getting back to studying. As we're living in the middle of information, floods, social media and the like, it's all too easy to spend our time in a state in which our memory in mind is not developing or recovering. It would be important to avoid this mental state.

When we study, we should give it our full attention and when we recover, we should give it our full attention as well. The most obvious point is that continuous review of social media or email is neither of those now a practical guidance. There are applications like Anqi that help you to optimize spaced repetition schedules. These apps are especially useful for memorization of simple things like terminology, but how to use spaced repetition and active recall with more complex topics. And, for example, test yourself about hands-on IT skills. One way to do this is to create a spreadsheet to list down concepts and procedures you need to learn with certification. This is usually the exam guide provided by the technology vendor, which lists all the topics which will be tested in the certification. Write down dates of your study plan in columns. Then while studying, take a topic from the list and try to explain out loud without relying on notes or external material.

Use a whiteboard or record yourself with a mobile phone if it makes recalling things easier. Or try to implement it, hands on, remember, learning by doing is the best way to learn, then use some kind of color coding to mark your progress while studying the topics. For example, if something was an easy market with green and if something needs a bit more practice market with yellow or maybe with red, if it was something that you need to do a lot more research on, this way you get a log and an overview of progress and see which topics need more rehearsal.

How The Mind Manages The Complexity

The third aspect of mind and memory, which I think is good to understand, especially as we're speaking about learning complex skills, is abstraction. As previously said, we have a working memory which could be thought of as the system to end long term memory, which could be thought of as system one based on the latest science our working memory can handle or remember only four things at once, or at least not much more than that. And once again, we cannot multitask. Using social media, email and other distractions will reserve these important memory slots and limit our capability to think of a single task as our conscious mind is not able to handle many pieces of information at once. We need to split complex concepts in pieces so that what we want to consciously think and process can fit in our limited working memory.

So the way we fit more complex concepts in our mind at once is that we break them down into abstractions. For example, if you're working in I.T., you're probably familiar with the concept of abstraction, as almost everything in it is an abstraction. We have processor's programming languages, more abstract programming languages on top of that APIs, cloud services and so on. This hierarchy of abstractions works well with how our memory is constructed as the higher level pieces work, as memory anchors neural pathways connected to lower level pieces of the concept and helps in polling related lower level pieces to working memory.

Another important point is what was mentioned when we spoke about stories. We remember things that are important and meaningful to us from this puzzle point of view. This means that we remember something better if we understand how it fits in the big picture understanding is super glue. The way we understand to remember complex concepts like information technology is that we form an abstraction hierarchy in which each piece has a logical, meaningful role in the whole. Moving back and forth in the abstraction not only helps us to see the trees in the forest, but reinforces the neural pathways that help us in multilevel thinking.

Why And How To Meta-Learn The Topic?

When we approach a new subject, it's useful to first do a bit of analysis on the subject. Scott Young in his book Ultra Learning, guides us to learn the subject before diving deeper into the topic. Examine the topic for a while and you'll be able to itemize. What are the concepts, facts and procedures that you will need to learn concepts, our ideas, abstractions or models that you need to understand so that you can analyze different situations. Facts are things you need to remember and commit to your memory. For example, specialized terminology procedures are things that you need to be able to do, preferably without too much conscious thinking.

The point is that there are different learning methodologies that suit best for each type of category. Concepts are best understood by reviewing or discussing them from different angles, trying them out in different environments, maybe writing about or teaching the concept or best of all, selling them and having to deal with thought, questions and counterarguments. Point being that testing out abstract concepts in the real world makes them antifragile with facts. You can use different memorization techniques. We don't go deep in here, but you can Google them easily. For example, try our keyword memory palace spaced repetition using active recall is the thing, and memorization tools like flash cards are a popular way for implementing it.

Flash cards are cards that have, for example, a term on one side and an explanation on the other side. These cards are an easy way to question yourself. There are applications like ANQI or even Kindle that have flash cards, applications that help you implement flash card routines and also optimize the cards so that if you repeatedly know something it's not asked as often. Flash cards could be a good way to learn terminology in it as well. If you're studying a topic in which terminology has a big role, consider writing down key terminology while you study and consider putting them into flash card applications for rehearsal going into procedures.

As I said before, learning has a specific effect. You learn what you practice. So if you need to learn programming or using certain cloud hands on nothing beats learning by facing the challenges hands on reveals your weak concepts and poor understanding of the facts. Getting to action is where everything starts, what makes the concepts and the facts stick, and also makes your learning meaningful. Without hands-on skills, your facts are meaningless and your concepts are full of holes.

What Are The Most Efficient Methods Of Learning?

It's easy to spend time on activities that feel productive but don't produce results. These are called vanity metrics. You might share my experience of reading an online learning chapter, thinking something totally different and waking up in realization that you didn't pay any attention to the chapter. If you invest your time in learning, it's better to invest it wisely. Well-known American entrepreneur and investor Rivkah shared his advice of investing time on learning as reading is faster than listening, doing is faster than reading. That's true. Getting hands on is the fastest and most efficient way to learn. This is not news. We get support from Confucius, a Chinese philosopher who lived 551 to four seventy nine BCE He said, I see and I forget. I hear and I remember. I do. And I understand.

Yet another insight from Edgartown found in his research. We remember 10 percent of what we read, 20 percent of what we hear, 30 percent of what we see, 50 percent of what we see and hear, 70 percent of what we say and 90 percent of what we say. And do we have a natural tendency to avoid getting hands on with something? We feel that we don't fully grasp something that feels uncertain. But learning by doing is the best way to learn. Learning needs effort, stop looking for shortcuts and get to work.

What Is The Best Way To Learn Different Kinds Of Topics?

Do you need more encouragement, let's reflect back on our discussion of concepts, facts and procedures. In the last hundred years or so, we've started to value cognitive capability, high education and smartness over working with your hearts in caring, emotional professions or hands on manual labor. This is changing organization structures are flattening agile methodologies or mainstream automation is replacing repetitive tasks. There's a more of a need for practical roles that can combine cognitive capability, caring and manual labor. As an example, in agile software development, relationship management, heart design, head and implementation hand are coming closer together. Now let's look at our approach for learning through this popular change management method and heart with our tendency to value our head, our cognitive capability, we usually approach learning the wrong way.

We start by trying to understand if it would be more practical to start with hands on doing something. Going Hands-On creates a relationship with the topic. It takes the heart on board without the personal experience. The facts we try to memorize are empty without meaning. It's easier to remember a fact if you have personal experience of it, you have a relationship with it. Now, when you have the personal hands on experience and meaningful relationship and language on the topic you're trying to learn, you can reflect on what this means and understand the related concepts much more deeply and permanently. Wisdom and insight comes from reflecting on our experiences. So go hands on first.

How To Tackle Different Kinds Of Material?

Now, let's think about how what we've learned reflects, depending on the kind of materials that you're consuming, reading books is fast. If you're preparing for certification that is well known, you will find a lot of courses that are focused on your chosen certification. However, certifications keep updating quite regularly, and books don't always follow the speed of change. Certification preparation books are also often quick shortcuts and don't actually explain the basics so that you would understand the topic if you are new to it. The best part of these certification books is that many have good practice tests and assignments that will help you get hands-on experience.

There are exceptions, but generally certification books work better as recap. If you already understand the topic or have previous experience of it, a book might be enough. Books are fast read and I would recommend considering using them as a quick recap at the end of your study days before the certification. Outside certification. There are good quality books, especially for real understanding, especially the deep theory of some topics. For example, if you're getting into machine learning and want to really understand the deep roots of the math behind it, nothing beats a good textbook on the topic. For this kind of deep understanding, I suggest reading books as the quickest path, but for more actionable learning goals.

For example, if you want to learn a new programming language, doing it hands on is a better approach. Online chapter. Online chapters are quite a popular option these days. There are plenty of sites that focus on technical skills. A cloud, guru.com, udemy plural sites, Bookra or even YouTube. Online learning is easily approachable and there are Books for everything you can imagine, especially for preparing for certifications. Availability has its hidden downside. Online learning is popular because people are looking for shortcuts and are eager to find ways to avoid putting in the effort learning really needs. It's easy to read chapters. It doesn't need much effort.

Reading online chapters is the most likely activity to become a vanity metric, something that feels productive but is not, reading online chapters is slow and not very efficient. However, there are good quality Books available and compared to certification preparation books, they usually really explain things from the basics. Many online chapter platforms also have labs that have very low thresholds to get in, but low threshold has its downside. If it's easy, it is easy to skip or to do without thinking about what you are doing and if there's no effort to. The learning response this week. That said, if you don't have previous experience with the topic you're trying to learn, a good online chapter is a good first step to take. Here's a tip.

Writing notes of an online chapter might be a good way to keep focus on the chapter counter to general understanding. Writing notes is shown not to be a very efficient method of learning because it's just copying things from working memory to paper and doesn't necessarily require effort that would activate the long term memory. But writing notes can help you keep focus on the chapter, and if you take notes by pencil and paper, it is so slow that it requires you to process and prioritize what is essential to write down which has some effect on long term learning. Another way to help with focus is to adjust the speed of the chapter to a bit higher speed so that it will require more attention to follow.

Classroom chapter is usually comparable to online chapter and its contents. However, compared to online chapters, classroom chapters enable you to focus. Many times you wouldn't take five days to focus on a topic without being able to join a classroom chapter. It's also really good because you learn from the questions that others raise and stories that the instructor shares. When you get to be face to face and see people's expressions and reactions, it helps you learn a lot better. It's also not tempting to skip the exercise while in the classroom. However, chapter and exercise might be made so fluent that you don't need to go through enough trouble to really learn the topic. But if your employer gives you an opportunity, grab it.

So it's recommended to take a classroom chapter every now and then, if possible. Maybe the biggest challenge of a classroom chapter is that being fully immersed in the classroom context makes it more challenging to bring the lessons to your own daily context. It's possible that much of the learning will stay in the classroom. That is called the transfer effect. It might be challenging to move the chapter from one environment to another for the best results. chapter or learning efforts should mimic real world use of skills as closely as possible. Yet again, another argument for learning. By doing online material browsing, many technology companies refer to their own online material for preparing for certification, and it's usually free. The quality does vary.

Sometimes it's good, sometimes it's bad. It will for sure be relevant for the certification. And it's a good idea to get experience and touch on the official source and documentation. Many times it's not really arranged best to suit for learning purposes, but in the best cases it provides hands on experiences or exercises and even less. And encourages learning by doing and in any case, working out with real documentation is closest to real work where you need the skill anyway, learning by doing. If you have a project of your own or tasked by someone, it can be really efficient. Learning vehicle. Ultimately, you learn by doing, learning, by doing is efficient because you will put in real effort. And if you really want to grasp something, there's no shortcut.

The best case is that you have a real project you need to get done, preferably with a deadline, with a real project. You'll have motivation to go through the challenge. Then you have a reason to go through documents or whatever material there is to get things done with a real goal and feedback of getting something solved, not just browsing through and thinking that you get it. The challenge is that it might take time. If you're new to the topic, you will make mistakes and you will need to come back to the intersection where you chose the wrong way. It's likely that you need or hopefully can rewrite or redo your project at least once after you have learned your lesson. This way of learning will just cover what you need and you might miss the bigger picture.

Learning by doing is a good way to start, but going through some other material will help to put things in context and reflect on the experience learning. By teaching, you will learn 90 percent of what you say and do active recall. As you remember, teaching is a very good way to learn. You need to really grasp your topic, be able to tell it in your own words and be able to answer tough questions. It will make the topics stick or think about what a requirement of selling a technical solution you have designed would affect your learning. You would get counterarguments and holes in your thinking will be exposed, committing to teach or share what you've learned or will learn with, for example, an Internal Tech Forum Meetup blog post. That's a really good way to intensify your learning efforts.

Surprising Effect Of Testing Yourself Early In The Process

Books and online Books provide practice tests for certification. What is the value of testing yourself and when should you do it? Obviously, as mentioned, you learn by trying to pull out something from memory. Spaced repetition is a way to do that, and tests are a good way to do active recall. It could be argued that testing should be done after studying towards the end of your studying sprint, maybe some days before the certification test. But there's also an interesting forward testing effect which states that testing can not only enhance what you've learned before space's repetition, but it can also make it easier to learn new information after testing.

Testing can enhance future learning even before there's any new learning done which to test. This effect is real. This might be due to the mind putting in the motivation and attention to find solutions to the open questions or challenges you could not solve when you tested yourself. Or it might be that the neural pathways and strategies related to looking for a solution to the topic in question are activated anyway. It might be useful to test yourself early in the learning process. And again, we come back to learning by doing learning, by utilizing an early testing approach.

If you try to implement something in your current professional role and you have challenges, it creates motivation and activates your brain for learning. So learning by doing might be the best way to utilize the forward testing effect. Testing is naturally also a good way to get a bit of a feeling for the test, how it's structured, type of questions and so on before you take the test. But avoid over preparation. It's not a huge mistake to fail a test. Real certification tests, they're good practice as well. Remember, win or learn.

Introduction To The Basis Of The System

Let's now look at how we put what we've learned into practice and start forming the super learning system. It's natural to procrastinate when we should focus on studying or like to maintain its safe equilibrium. Approaching something new that we don't fully grasp yet is a threat to ourselves, and it can make us anxious. Hence, our mind easily tries to move our focus away from studying social media being the drug of choice for distraction nowadays. Or you might be familiar with sudden urges to start cleaning the house when you should be studying. Finding distractions easily becomes a habit. To avoid this, we need a better habit, a good system of studying that puts the best practices together so that instead of inventing distractions, our mind starts to look out for our next studying session.

A good system removes uncertainty and gives clear guidance on what exactly to do. Clear guidance helps our mind with procrastination by lowering the risk of paralysis by analysis, continuous loop of pondering whether there's a better way to approach the topic. We should start our search for a good system with something that is shown to work at risk where animals are, we're naturally wired to look for reasons why something might not work. But the better way is to look for what has already been shown to work and scale. That one such system that's gaining more and more popularity and credibility is called the Pomodoro method.

The Pomodoro method is the core. We built our system on Pomodoro. Its name comes from a Pomodoro kitchen timer. The idea of a pomodoro is that we set the kitchen timer or some other modern timer to twenty five minutes and commit to work on the task at hand for the time with full focus to shut out all other distractions, then have five minutes of break and then do the next pomodoro. This system really works. Twenty five minutes is not too long of a time to commit to focusing on one thing. We're not made to multitask.

Context switching is productivity poison. It can take up to ten minutes to switch between tasks and get your working memory fully in use again. As there's residue from the last effort for a while, Pomodoro also helps to lower the threshold of approaching new big topics that you feel anxious about. Pomodoro helps by enabling us to focus on the process, not the goal. You can check what you've done from your to-do list when twenty five minutes of work is done, which is the goal. Not when some huge task is completed and you get your shot of dopamine, which helps you to focus again. Pomodoro is based on time boxing. Instead of a task list, you time box pre-defined time to work on something.

It's especially good for bigger chunks of work that can't be done in one sitting, such as learning or preparing for a certificate. The time doesn't have to be twenty five minutes. The perfect time depends on your attention span. So our suggestion is that you test how long you're able to focus and alter the time up or down from twenty five minutes and maybe set a goal to expand it over time. Some people use forty five minutes to focus and fifteen minutes of break. The Pomodoro method gives you the rhythm of studying the mind's focused mode and relaxation break diffused mode. It's a good habit or ritual and using it to teach your mind to focus when the timer starts. Some other practical tips for using the Pomodoro method are to shut out all possible distractions.

If something important pops up in your mind, write it down to get it out of your head and continue your effort. Don't fill your mind with other tasks while on break. Remember the cost of context switching. Keep some of the journal or to do list of your sessions so you can mark them done and get your shot of dopamine. Give yourself a reward after completing your sessions to enhance habit formation, completing itself as a reward. But some like to have coffee on breaks. Enter your session with a calm mind, breathe for a while, write down possibly distracting thoughts or to do elements and rehearse. What is the focus of the session before you start?

Scheduling The System For Optimal Results

Now, if Pomodoro is the basis of our system, we need to make using it a habit first. Let's have a look at the Eisenhower matrix of planning and decision making. It divides things in important and not so important, and on the other hand, on urgent and not so urgent levels. Studying, learning, sharpening your saw is important, but not urgent. It's easy to focus on important and urgent tasks and decide to study later. But that later never comes. To avoid this trap of being reactive and filling our days with urgent tasks, we need to schedule time for proactive efforts. This is especially important for our learning efforts, as studying is not something you can put on your task list and check down after a single burst.

Learning larger topics needs recurring focus sessions of deep effort. As you remember, you're never ready, and learning should be a part of your daily effort and part of your professional identity. You should plan how much time of your professional life you use for studying and focus on using that time. Well, not that much on the goal of getting the next cert. Now, you might also remember that time and place are important for habit formation. When we use the Pomodoro method as our basis for the system, the question is how many pomodoro a week or a day will you invest in learning? I recommend that you plan which days, in which time you study and how many sessions you do, and keep that schedule in routine to form a habit out of it. Mornings are usually a good time for focused efforts before doing anything else.

Our minds are clear. There's also not so much competition in our time in the early mornings. In addition, for most of us, it's also rhythmically the time our mind is at its best state of learning. You can consider waking up a bit earlier to ensure the time for studying. Doing proactive work first thing in the morning also helps by giving you a related dopamine shot which drives action and focus for the rest of the day. In the morning when the day plans, how much you can invest. If it's one, two or three pomodoro sessions, three to five times a week, don't think about the goal, how much action you're able and should invest. We have a biorhythm that goes in about 90 minutes.

Ninety minutes or three. Pomodoro could be a good candidate for daily goals, whether it's one, three or five times a week. This is also what Eriksson's study on deliberate practice showed as optimal. Consider this. Doing thirty minutes of studying five days a week would count to fourteen days, seven five hour days of studying a year, which is almost three work weeks of high quality focused studying a year or doing ninety minutes of learning five days a week would count to forty two days or two full months of full time, very focused time on studying. I bet average college students don't get more than that of focused quality studying time of year. Imagine where this might lead your career in five or ten years.

Inside The System

Now we have time and process for our daily learning effort. Lastly, let's dig into how to structure the content of our Pomodoro sessions. We've already chosen our topic or mid-term goal, which is not too far, but needs a bit of push, effort and focus. Our next certification with the certification is quite easy to find a certification exam guide that lists the topics we need to master. Here we can see the certification exam guide for Google Cloud Associate Cloud Engineer Certification. It lists higher level themes covered and goes down into each individual skill we should acquire. How I do it is I copy and paste the exam guide to a spreadsheet. Here I have my sheet with some formatting to make it look a bit nicer.

I've added the weeks and dates in the columns so I can use the spreadsheet keeping journey of my studying efforts. In this example, I've decided to invest three twenty five pomodoro one and a half hours each morning for studying. I've decided to mark finishing a pomodoro session on my sheet with X next. I would do a bit of reattach on available materials. If you feel that you are familiar with the topics and have good experience working hands-on with the area of certification already, you might choose to skip the materials and decide to start rehearsing and testing the topics. Hands on one by one from the list, rehearsing by doing.

I have some experience with other clouds, but Google Cloud platform was totally new to me, so I felt that I needed an introduction to Google Cloud in the concepts first before getting down to hands-on practice. So I decided to look for a chapter or a book to give me the first acquaintance on the topic. Browsing through the Internet, I found that cloud guru.com seems to have CGP Books as well as you, Grammy.com and also Bookra offering chapters for Google Cloud. Then looking into Amazon.com, I found that there's actually a pretty good official book about GCP certification. Reading is faster than reading, so I decided that I will use the book as the basis for my learning. It seemed to have a nice overview and also step by step guides for trying things, hands on which I decided to follow while reading.

To get familiar with Google Cloud Interface in my sheet, I decided to use the following method. I marked the first round of reading and following hands on with Blue. Then I did a second round without the book, trying to remember or implement the topics at each row. If it feels easy, I mark them with green, meaning I'm done with the topic. If I had to check the correct answer from the book or felt uncertain, I marked it with yellow. And if the topic at some roll was something I felt needed to investigate more, I marked it with red. I repeated this for some rounds, skipping the green rows until I thought that the spreadsheet was green enough. There were still some yellow rows marking, but I didn't mind that.

Example Of The Daily Grind

Here's my routine or ritual I did every morning after I woke up while studying for a Google certification, it was during the covid lockdown, which helped a bit to keep the routine. I usually wake up quite early, six to seven a.m. After waking up, I stretch and do some bodyweight exercises like push ups or pull ups, take some coffee and take a cold shower before starting out. Then I usually put on some instrumental music on headphones that help me to focus, which also works nicely as a cue to start the learning habit. I don't check my email before I finish the session and I have my phone on airplane mode. Not that anyone usually disturbs me this early in the morning anyway. I have a clean laptop, desktop and no extra applications open.

Then I take out my Excel sheet and open the required material so that everything is ready. I sit down, breathe and rehearse the focus for the day. I set up a timer for 25 minutes and started going through the material and hands-on practices. I remind myself not to hurry and to focus on the process. If I feel pressure while going through the material and hands on practices, I slow down and remind myself to take the time it takes to understand something. Research has shown that pushing too much moves attention to conscious systems, too. If you find yourself pushing too heavily, it might make sense to slow down a bit to take the super processing capabilities of System One in use, especially if you're doing something creative or utilizing learned capabilities of System one.

Also, getting in the flow requires you to relax, remember the flow cycle, first struggle and second, relax. When twenty five minutes is done, I stop immediately. It's easier to continue. Something that was not finished as an open loop stays active in my mind. While the finish loop will disappear more quickly during the break. I don't check on social media or email. I stand up. I walk a bit, I drink some water, and visit the men's room. If necessary. I might stretch or do some squats or pushups. I might as well read out from the window to relax my eyes. And when the break is done I go back to work and continue where I left off.

After three sessions I'm done. This is usually before nine a.m. I've done proactive work first thing in the morning and I'm energetic, ready for the day and all the reactive work and socializing ahead, especially studying about the topics that I need in my professional role. Put some order and structure in the information overload and complexity that haunts me and it releases energy. Next day I'll do the same and the next in a couple of weeks. I wonder how much I've gone through and learned how material that originally seemed like too much to even approach, I internalized. And how much of that now seems obvious. I really recommend this approach for you too.

Conclusion

Now, we've covered the theory strategies and techniques of learning it skills at last. Now it's time for you to get started, which is the most important skill. You rarely get motivated sitting on the sofa. There is a certain friction of starting anything new. We want to be in control and there's a natural tension in approaching something new, something that we don't yet manage and feel uncertain about. To overcome this friction, Mark Manson in his book Subtle Art of Not Giving a—, recommends his rule of just doing something. The point of just doing something is that we have this misunderstanding about motivation. We think that we're likely to commit to action only if we feel a certain level of motivation.

That is an emotional inspiration. We think that we first get emotional inspiration, then feel motivation and take action only when motivated. But the reality is that it also works the other way around. Action drives inspiration, which creates motivation. Action is not just the effect of motivation, but also the cause of it. Just do something if this isn't true, to get you moving. As the last stop of this chapter, I want to share the five second rule. Five seconds rule is a concept introduced by Mel Robbins. Five second rule says that if you have an instinct to act, you must just start within five seconds or your brain will kill the instinct.

After five seconds, you start to come up with objections and your mind breaks and it takes over control. So when you feel hesitation towards doing something that you know you should do. Countdown five, four, three, two, one. Go and start. By the way, my goal is to make the chapter as good as possible. Getting your feedback on this Book would be really important to me for developing this further. If you don't mind spending a moment and leaving a review of the Book, that would mean a lot to me and I would really appreciate your effort.

Don't miss out!

Visit the website below and you can sign up to receive emails whenever SHAKRUDDIN KHAN publishes a new book. There's no charge and no obligation.

https://books2read.com/r/B-A-DUGBB-JVSZC

BOOKS 2 READ

Connecting independent readers to independent writers.

Also by SHAKRUDDIN KHAN

The Smart Way To Personal Finance Success
Goal Setting 101 Achieve More Goals Than Ever! Faster!
Blockchain Masterclass for Businesses and Corporations
Master Your Mindset & Brain Framestorm Your Way To Success
Manipulation Techniques: How Can We Influence People's Thoughts And Behaviors
Leadership How To Influence, Inspire And Impact As A Leader
Learn How To Create A Safe Working Environment For Your Team
Productivity Hacks For Easily Distractible Entrepreneurs
IT / Non-IT Recruiter Training To Become A Recruiter (Junior)

www.ingramcontent.com/pod-product-compliance
Lightning Source LLC
Chambersburg PA
CBHW070855160726
48004CB00003B/1090